Beckett and Myth

Irish Studies

BECKETT and MYTH

An Archetypal Approach

MARY A. DOLL

SYRACUSE UNIVERSITY PRESS

The paper used in this publication meets the minimum requirements of American National Standard for Information Sciences—Permanence of Paper for Printed Library Materials, ANSI Z39.48-1984. ∞™

Library of Congress Cataloging-in-Publication Data

Doll, Mary Aswell.
    Beckett and myth: an archetypal approach/Mary A.
    Doll. — 1st ed.
    p. cm. — (Irish studies)
    Bibliography: p.
    Includes index.
    ISBN 0-8156-2447-6 (alk. paper)
    1. Beckett, Samuel, 1906–   —Criticism and
interpretation.   2. Archetype (Psychology) in
literature.   3. Myth in literature.   I. Title.   II. Series:
Irish studies (Syracuse, N.Y.).
PR6003.E282Z6255 1988   88-19746
848'.91409—dc19   CIP

Manufactured in the United States of America

This book is dedicated to my three Williams.

MARY ASWELL DOLL has written about Beckett, myth, and archetypal images in several publications and has lectured on these topics at conferences in the U.S. and abroad. She is the coeditor of *In the Shadow of the Giant* (1988), a collection of the letters of her father, who edited the posthumous works of Thomas Wolfe. She has taught in both the New York and the California state university systems. Currently, she lives, writes, and teaches in southern Louisiana.

Contents

Illustrations

Acknowledgments

Extracts from Samuel Beckett's *Ends and Odds*, *Ill Seen Ill Said*, *Three Novels*, and *Collected Poems in French and English* are reprinted with the permission of Grove Press. Extracts from *Ends and Odds: Dramatic Pieces* by Samuel Beckett are reprinted with the permission of Faber and Faber Ltd., London. Permission to quote material from Samuel Beckett's *Ill Seen Ill Said*, *Three Novels*, *Collected Poems 1930–1978* is granted by John Calder Ltd., London. Portions of chapter 4 have appeared in "Rites of Story: The Old Man at Play," in *Myth and Ritual in the Plays of Samuel Beckett*, edited by Katherine H. Burkman, and are reprinted with the permission of Fairleigh Dickinson University Press. Permission to reprint portions of Mary A. Doll's "Demeter and Myth," an article forthcoming in *Journal of Beckett Studies*, no. 11, is granted by John Calder Ltd., London. Portions of chapter 5 have appeared as "Walking and Rocking in *Footfalls* and *Rockaby*," in *Make Sense Who May*, edited by Robin J. Davis and Lance St. John Butler, and are reprinted with the permission of Barnes and Noble Books, Totowa, N.J., and Colin Smyth Ltd., Buckinghamshire, U.K.

The following colleagues in the Beckett Society have been supportive and helpful to me in ways they probably do not know: Walter Asmus, Martha Fehsenfeld, Stan Gontarski, Sighle Kennedy, James Knowlson, Dougald McMillan, Peter Murphy, Lois More Overbeck, and Rubin Rabinovitz. Special thanks go to Beckett colleagues Susan Brienza and Katherine Burkman for their critical insights and warm personal friendship over the years. Thanks, too, to Dierdre Bair, Judith Dearlove, and William Mueller, for help and inspiration of various sorts along the way, way back. I also wish to acknowledge George Koenig and Josette Melzer for their parts in helping me with translation. For directing this manuscript in its early dissertation stages I wish to thank David L. Miller, whose writings continue to inspire my thinking. I also owe a great debt to Richard Fallis for seeing this manuscript into publication.

Abbreviations

In quoting Beckett's works in the text the following abbreviations have been used, and all references will be to these editions:

B   *Bram van Velde.* New York: Grove Press, 1960.

C   *Company.* New York: Grove Press, 1980.

Cas   *Cascando* in *Cascando and Other Short Dramatic Pieces.* New York: Grove Press, 1969.

C&G *Come and Go* in *Cascando and Other Short Dramatic Pieces.* New York: Grove Press, 1969.

D   "Denis Devlin" (Review of 'Intercessions'), *transition* no. 27 (April–May 1938):289–94.

E   "The End" in *Stories & Texts for Nothing.* New York: Grove Press, 1967.

EB   "Echo's Bones" in *Collected Poems in French and English.* New York: Grove Press, 1961.

Emb *Embers* in *Krapp's Last Tape & Other Dramatic Pieces.* New York: Grove Press, 1960.

End   *Endgame.* New York: Grove Press, 1958.

F   *Footfalls* in *Ends and Odds: Eight New Dramatic Pieces.* New York: Grove Press, 1976.

HD   *Happy Days.* New York: Grove Press, 1961.

HH   "Henri Hayden, homme-peintre." *Henri Hayden Recent Paintings* (Catalogue). London: Waddington Galleries (February 1959):2.

I   *Ill Seen Ill Said.* New York: Grove Press, 1981.

K   *Krapp's Last Tape.* New York: Grove Press, 1960.

L   Letter to Axel Kaun (September 1937). Dartmouth College Library, Hanover, New Hampshire.

M   *Molloy* in *Three Novels by Samuel Beckett.* New York: Grove Press, 1965.

Mur *Murphy.* New York: Grove Press, 1957.

N   *Not I* in *Ends and Odds.* New York: Grove Press, 1976.

OI   *Ohio Impromptu* in *Rockaby and Other Short Pieces.* New York: Grove Press, 1981.

P   *Proust.* New York: Grove Press, 1931.

PD   "Papini's Dante" (Review), *The Bookman* 87 (Christmas 1934):14.

Pein "Peintres de l'empêchement," *Derrière le miroir,* nos. 11, 12 (June 1948):3–7.

PV   "Poetry Is Vertical." (manifesto) in *transition* 21 (March 1932):148–49.

R   *Rockaby* in *Rockaby and Other Short Pieces.* New York: Grove Press, 1981.

RIP   "Recent Irish Poetry," *The Bookman* 77 (August 1934):241–42.

TT   *That Time* in *Ends and Odds.* New York: Grove Press, 1976.

U   *The Unnamable* in *Three Novels.* New York: Grove Press, 1965.

W   *Waiting for Godot.* New York: Grove Press, 1954.

Beckett and Myth

Introduction

A survey of the Beckett criticism of the seventies reveals an overwhelming emphasis on Beckett's concern with philosophy. Beckett's use of ideas such as rationalism, pessimism, or existentialism—shaped according to their formalist, absurdist, or deconstructive molds—has been well documented.[1] Language studies, including manuscript investigation and stylistics, are also prime approaches to Beckett's work.[2] A similar survey of mythic studies of Beckett, however, reveals a very different story. Over the past twenty-five years, only six critics have made myth the center of their focus on Beckett.[3]

This critical gap is surprising, for a mythic rather than a philosophic approach to being resonates throughout Beckett's personal letters and critical writings. He refers, for instance, to the undersurface of all things (L) to the invasion of surface by ground, to the evocation of the unsaid by the said (D, 293). A mythic view of ground and undersurface suggests a relation between earth and underworld, alive mythically but hidden to logical thought processes. For Beckett's characters life is hell, nothing going on forever. As the Unnamable—an unnamed, unborn "character" in an early Beckett novel—puts it (referring to the process of living), "the thing stays where it is, nothing changes, within it, outside it, apparently, apparently" (U, 370). But below surfaces and between the cracks of consciousness an other nonrational world of myth and psychic energy seeps through. With Beckett, as with the Chinese poets, nothing means something; shadows hide layers; voices echo; and objects, like jars, contain depth. Hell's negativism becomes an empty space, inside of which images, objects, and bodies live differently; that is, imaginally, mythically.

What *Beckett and Myth* proposes is a reevaluation of Beckett's work based on a poetics of myth. Quests to and from, characters who are archetypes not stereotypes, constant variations upon sames: all imply an insistence—like that of myth—that we return to the ground of being. Myths, we could say, have a curious Beckettian quality. As stories that never come to an end, myths build upon basic patterns, giving an opportunity to create endings and to re-create beginnings. As one lexicon puts it, myths are stories told to those who do not listen.[4] In such a way, Beckett's work is resoundingly mythic. An old man with greatcoat

1

and stick appears many, many times in the course of the Beckett canon, repeating words heard earlier, obsessed by images seen earlier. Women appear in black gowns or tattered wraps, disturbed out of their minds. This constant drumming of sameness-with-slight-variation into the pages of fiction and drama seems perverse. It is as if Beckett knows readers and listeners were not attending well enough the first time and so need to be told again, and again, or as if what appeared once is of such urgency that it must be seen again, heard again, in another key. Eye, ear, and mouth (open to receive the older words) become like orifices of Hades, where the other speaks. But what is this other speaking of myth that must be spoken so often? What is it Beckett says?

It seems that Beckett presents what Carl Jung calls "modern man in search of soul." For fifty years Beckett's work has focused on soul-searching—the topic, as well, of myth and of depth psychology. Beckett takes us to various places, where soul—glimpsed but not found—is felt at its zero point. Empty rooms and ancient ruins become places that induce a thinking mind to cease for a moment its tiresome habit of figuring things out, always to conclusion, and to feel, for a change. There, in the space that emptiness affords, the living soul suffers. There, the searched-for soul lives. Beckett shows that we have absolutely no choice in the matter of going back to this other place. The venture is entirely beyond our willing and has nothing whatever to do with heroics. Our life depends on it, however; for to journey to that emptiness is to rediscover the forgotten soul.

To chart this venture into psychic depth I connect Beckett explicitly with another twentieth-century excavator of soul, Carl Jung. Jung's work with schizophrenics demonstrated just how fractured the modern Western, rational condition can become, with its insistence on excessive thought at the expense of psychic life. Writing in prewar Switzerland, Jung feared that a larger schizophrenia was plaguing humankind in the name of eugenics. Calling itself a purification of the races, eugenics—Jung predicted—would eventually erupt in the form of war and would manifest the disease of purified thought (Naziism) in atrocious acts of literalism. Jung wrote of modernity's "black collective shadow," which neglects, ignores, represses, or otherwise puts to sleep a deeper, undiscovered self.[5] Jung's search for self, or soul, took him not to the lofty phrases of statesmen, nor to exquisite scientific mechanisms, nor to systems of purity and perfection; but into the psychoses of his patients who, because they suffered their alienating condition, could not function. Oddly, by shutting out "reality," these patients lived totally among the archaic remnants of the unconscious, the emotionally charged picture-language of dreams, myths, and primitive rites.

Jung's research into wisdom literatures, alchemical symbol systems, and myth offers an answer as to why the modern condition is so disintegrated. In premodern traditions Jung found a more complete universe, where the soul, fed by its own shadows, was nourished. Premodern peoples did not repress the black shadow because they embodied it figuratively (not literally) in grotesque forms, unfamiliar shapes, unacceptable thoughts, and obscene ideas. As part of the collectivity, the premodern soul was also part of the shadow and lived in it. In time, and to every person, as surely as night came, so came this other shadowed existence, symbolically, in shared cultural patterns. Jung moved away from Freud's ego theory, with its purifying, singling-out tendency, insisting that instinct, feeling, fantasy, and sickness are the real material—or matter—of being's roots. When modern Western egotism ignores such roots, Jung claimed, the consequence is an ignoring of the soul's connection with darkness. Jung called his a psychology of soul, not of ego, in recognition of a power that lies behind rational or egoistic thought—a power that, when repressed, wreaks carnage but when allowed to flourish, connects humankind.

Beckett's mythic writings take our modern egos, fractured by excessive rationalism, into just such radical "matter." Readers and viewers of Beckett find it impossible to respond to the texts intellectually, only. Like dreams or nightmares, the texts require us to live in them. Deepest feelings get riled, truths get contradicted, uncertainty prevails. Inside this process, forgotten but familiar, we become stirred by unconsciousness and feel ourselves living differently, as never before. More than any writer of our time, Beckett makes this other reality the "soul" center of his concern. His avowed purpose, as he has stated, in fact, is for us to know the night and see the shadow.[6]

If Beckett makes anything clear it is this: that the old logic of the old heroic quest pattern won't do. The myth of the hero, for Beckett, is not a structuring principle, as it was for Joyce. Beckett's quest does not reaffirm the Ulyssean ego, does not give the hero his boon, does not bring full circle, back home again, problems raised in the beginning and resolved at the end. Beckett's quest does none of this; rather, his mythic sense fragments the ego, breaking authority away from its stranglehold on truth. Instead of a heroic monomyth of departure-encounter-return, Beckett inverts the pattern. His intent, as one critic puts it, is to "undo."[7] I term Beckett's pattern one of regressing-encountering-sensing, with emphasis on the present participle, never-ending progressive verb. This suggests that in Beckett's pattern, as in myth, one cannot depart before one returns; and that when one does return to the roots of being, one is in the midst of such enchantment that one must relinquish intellect for sense. Then the senses come alive, replacing mere common or willed sense, and time returns to the present tense. Beckett's connection with myth is thus with language roots and psychic roots, with undersurfaces and interstices, with poetries of the soul.

My approach in this book is to argue, as other postmodern critics do, that the serious issues of our time require a communication that breaks form. The forms that once held our thought systems together logically, sequentially, hierarchically, no longer speak to our understanding. Ours is a world governed by uncertainty, illogic, and pluralism. When—as Nietzsche claimed—God died, and—as Yeats described—the center fell apart, an entire tradition of thinking smashed into pieces: from Christian theology, Newtonian science, and Darwinian evolutionary theory, through to utilitarianism, classical liberalism, and ego psychology. A wave of recent writings in postmodernism suggests that although the old thought systems are inadequate for our time, new paths can be found to guide our groping. In fields other than literature, David Miller's *Christs*, for instance, breaks form with monotheism and the pietistic view orthodox Christianity presents. Ilya Prigogine's *Order Out of Chaos* finds fault with Newtonian science and its spawning of the scientific method. Similarly, Carolyn Merchant's *Death of Nature* challenges the hierarchy implicit in Darwinian evolution. And James Hillman's *Re-Visioning Psychology*, in insisting on a psychological rather than a scientific method, writes in an episodic manner (self-styled as "helter skelter") which offers an alternative to heady academic discourse.

In literature, the breaking of form is best characterized by deconstruction theory. According to this theory, a text—constructed by an author whose life contains a definite history and a clear bias—is reconstructed by a reader whose life differs from that of the author and whose perspective is framed differently. A reader becomes part of a context when reading a book. But what is particularly startling about deconstruction theory is its insistence that a text—in the process of becoming reconstructed by a reader—must also undergo change and assume a life of its own that is different from that which its author intended. Deconstruction theory thus undermines authority in its most literal sense. It further undermines a clean Cartesian split between author and reader, subject and object, text and context. As J. Hillis Miller puts it, "rather than surveying the text with sovereign command from outside (deconstruction) remains caught within the activity in the text it retraces."[8]

But these postmodern approaches are not without method. Rather, the writings that I have cited celebrate new opportunities emerging from broken forms. In dethroning the central positions that God, man, science, and logic have occupied for centuries in Western thought systems, postmodern critics challenge us to see that the old forms were haughty. Their arrogant hierarchy and merciless logic pretended to a certainty that closed us off not only from horizontal relationships with one another but also from vertical descents into the self.

My critical approach to Beckett's work borrows from the implications of postmodern thinking, of which deconstruction theory is a part. Like the postmodernists, I see Beckett debunking the systems of Western culture that perpetuate a closed vision. Like the deconstructionists, I see Beckett presenting contextual encounters in every text, communicating from within the shattered pieces. Consistent with this postmodern, deconstructive approach, I break form with traditional Jungian criticism as it has too often been applied to literary texts, reifying characters into stereotypes of archetypes. Jung's depth psychology became, in the hands of modernist critics, just another system, like that of Kantian idealism, that owed little to the phenomena of images, patterns, or sounds. My claim, on the contrary, is that Beckett's work lends itself wonderfully to a mythopoetic method precisely because it breaks form. It not only eschews the established systems of Western philosophy, it also rejects such other systems as Jungian criticism that impose themselves upon texts in gridlike certainty. In so doing, Beckett's work redefines what is old into new moments, neither denying the past nor clinging to it. Rather, Beckett's poetics of myth allows us to see patterns, and to hear patterns, and to read patterns afresh.

Besides the obvious formal qualities of quests and archetypes, at least two additional qualities characterize Beckett's mythopoetics, or poetics of myth. The first has to do with Beckett's style of textual speaking, which is fluid. Language itself is fluid. Same words mean different things in different contexts; same sounds mean different words; contradictions are constant; old words are resurrected; old words give new words new meaning. What this style accomplishes is a tremendous sense of an unstable structure. Yet—and this is the point—there is precision amidst fluidity. Critics have termed it differently. Rubin Rabinovitz describes it as a repeating helix pattern.[9] Stan Gontarski refers to a musical structure.[10] Susan Brienza notes the tracing of mandala shapes.[11] These descriptions are helpful. But perhaps Moran in his moronic mindlessness at the end of his journey back home expresses the pattern best. Moran is fascinated by the dance bees make as they come and go from their hive. He talks about the complicated figures traced in flight, the same figure accompanied by different hums. He wonders what the dance is saying, what the hums say. And then he makes this observation: "For the bees did not dance at any level, haphazard, but there were three or four levels, always the same, at which they danced. And if I were to tell you what these levels were, and what the relations between them, for I had measured them with care, you would not believe me" (M, 169). Of course, we can't believe Moran any more than Jung could believe his schizophrenic patients. Yet the observation is trenchant and provides a metaphoric way of thinking about Beckett's mythic language. It is a thinking that is, as Beckett might describe, "precisely fluid."

A second quality of Beckett's mythopoetics is its centeredness on objects. In myth one thinks of the power objects give to the gods and goddesses. Through his lyre Hermes achieved forgiveness. With a stone Rhea saved her son Zeus from chronic engulfment. It was the plucking of a flower that struck Hades' heart and spurred his drastic deed. In each of these situations an object brings about change and gives to subjects a greater depth of feeling. Something in the It, not the I, speaks to soul. This power from the object is integral to Beckett's texts.

Stamp and picture albums speak wordlessly to deeper recesses of being. Stones are sucked for comfort. Stools invade their woodenness so completely into wood-ened imaginations that in "The End" and "Cascando" the narrator feels himself turned to pieces of old wood, drifting along with the tide. Here objects endow imagination with a literally new sense. One does not imagine by abstraction; one imagines concretely, by interacting imaginatively with objects. This is literalism at an other level, a level that mythically understands where magical powers are placed. The place resides not in the sure confines of egoistic thought, but in the mute and layered depths of things. [12]

When, therefore, Beckett says that the old ego dies hard (P, 10) he is sug-gesting two ideas about the search for soul. On the one hand, this search is un-dertaken by an ego hardened to change. Beckett's names for these characters re-veal his attitude toward them: they are hams, full of crap; they are morons. On the other hand, the statement suggests that an old ego dies with great diffi-culty—hard—and with suffering. This second reading implies that the dying of ego will give birth to the soul: that the difficult death of one gives life to the other. If, then, the texts cause us to suffer confusion, Beckett has achieved his purpose; for only when we feel confused and wracked do we begin to sense our egos in a rack with soul. [13] Only then can Beckett's mythic dimension truly speak.

I discuss Beckett's mythic exploration of soul by describing three stages or types of consciousness. These three types crisscross in Beckett's texts, as they do in mine. Scenes or images from one work concerning one type of consciousness appear in one chapter of this study and later in another. Such a sow-and-reap strategy is necessary, I argue, because of the implicitly mythic quality of the texts, where no image, no pattern, no figure or type of consciousness exists in solitary splendor. Understanding comes from replication, echoing-back, deep-ening, thickening. Each implies another. Each type describes the old ego dying hard. The old man, for example, Beckett's favorite character type, is egoism ri-gidified by excessive rationalism. This type is characterized by the myth of Cronus, which we Westerners must confront if we are ever to go beyond a re-pressive need to swallow imagination, as Cronus did metaphorically when he swallowed his children. A second type is the old woman, a Demeter figure, op-posite from the old man but akin to him in her hardened anger. This myth forces us to confront that which hardens the ability to respond to situations we cannot control. A third type is that of the child—the swallowed or buried other. Be-cause of its place in beginnings, the child is what an old ego must regress to—not by figuring things out but by figuring things in: into the play of words, into memory gaps, into objects, even into silence. The child is what is taut beneath the lines of reasoning. These three types of consciousness focus the three myths of this study: the myth of Narcissus and Echo (chapter 3), the myth of Cronus (chapter 4), and the myth of Demeter (chapter 5). Chapter 6 applies Beckett's poetics of myth, outlined in chapter 1, to key objects, which in *Company* and *Ill Seen Ill Said* take on totemic importance. By focusing on objects rather than subjects, on Its not I's, Beckett's characters begin the approach to being, beyond the confines of ego. Seen outside the body in the cosmos or within the mind in memory, being (or soul) displaces ego. The I is put behind the eye, to where seeing acquires an interior sense.

Finally, I subtitle this book "an archetypal approach"—as opposed to a deconstructionist or a Jungian approach—to suggest that my interest is not in schools of critical or psychological thought, but in method. Beckett insists that art has nothing whatever to do with clarity (D, 293); in fact, he proposes that language be released from bondage inside its own system. He connects the roots of language with music and painting, because these allow for great black pauses (L). There, in the black silence, something happens to the listener not hard of hearing. A mystery invades the moment. Beckett's proposal is radical, in the way an archetypal approach is radical, for it is an urging to let go the literal way and to return instead to what one can neither see nor hear clearly: a return to the archetypes. But rather than reifying archetypes into such Jungian terms as anima, animus, or trickster, Beckett's archetypal return takes away labels (which are, after all, only literalisms). His texts subvert, destroy, deviate; readers are torn from their safe resting places into the black pause. An archetypal approach to Beckett's texts is not interested in identifying archetypes but rather in allowing the coarse and violent images to come forth of themselves. For there, in the black pause, strange textual figures and images force us to acknowledge their otherness, and in otherness lives the soul. Beckett's regressive quest into empty spaces thus truly accomplishes a miracle. Things, sensed as if for the first time, open eyes to shadow seeing for the first time. Ears, newly opened in the wondering bewilderment of doubleness sounded in language or not sounded in silence, hear differently. We may not in Beckett's texts find our souls; but we may, at the very least, begin a journey that moves us from the rocky shore of egoism into the waters of all time.

1   A Poetics of Myth

Between the late twenties and the fifties Beckett wrote approximately sixteen pieces of criticism. These pieces are remarkable for the urgency of their prodding and for the consistency of their view, as well as for the light they shed on Beckett's own artistic intention. A further aspect of these critical writings is Beckett's ground-breaking recognition that the field of painting had much to offer the field of writing. The canvasses of such little-known painters as Jack B. Yeats, Henri Hayden, and the Dutch brothers Geer and Bram van Velde, Beckett said, assault a viewer's eyes with objects so strange that they seem to partake of a reality all their own. Praising this new object-centered art, Beckett wrote in one review that seeing objects aids in the process of seeing the self as a more complex multiplicity of layers (RIP, 241).

Beckett's critical writings are central for an understanding of the role of art in the quest for selfhood. They lay the groundwork for a totally new aesthetic which rejects Aristotle's unities, Clive Bell's right-mindedness,[1] and Joyce's genius. Indeed, such an aesthetic can be defined in any number of ways and with reference to any number of genres—to gambling, for instance, or to the unstable structures of quantum physics, even to indigence.[2] My purpose, however, is to illuminate Beckett's art with reference to myth.

Three features distinguish a poetics of myth from a poetics of logic, making the former radical: true, that is, to its roots in poetry and psyche rather than in reason and mind. First, a mythopoetics must step back from so-called normal perception in order to establish an other way. Beckett defines such an act of regression by negatives: it cannot be seen clearly, it is not reached through ordinary sense perception, it is not understood by means of logic, it cannot be named. A poetics of myth thus contains anomalies, contradictions, and variations—endless variations—that shift the foundation beneath the perceiver, such that no single position or mindset can serve as guidepost. This first feature of a mythopoetic introduces the viewer of an artwork if not to the world of possibility at least to the limitations of the world of certainty.

A second feature of a poetics of myth is to prepare space for an encounter between viewer and object. The beholder of the art object—character, reader, artist—is placed in an initiatory position, seeking only to understand It, how It is. Its other reality makes itself felt intensely, while being understood only dimly—veiled from ego's logic. Its moment of presentation thus involves two dimensions, or axes, from the viewer or listener. A horizontal axis, of ego consciousness and rationality, tries to figure things out; a vertical axis, of psychic depth, dream, and myth, presents figures and images. Beckett suggests that if one were to live on two axes at once, in touch with both the vertical and horizontal dimensions of being, one would live as never before, "co-axing" (HH, 2). Not only would one live within two axes (that of the rational and that of the psychic zone), doubling sense perception and confounding sense—one would also sharpen awareness, as one sharpens an axe. Such doubling, unusual for ego aesthetics accustomed to center-stage literalism, introduces a wholly different factor into art.

Beckett's poetic is mythic to the extent that he does not separate himself as the artist from his characters or his audience. All of us become readers of the same myth. All of us are artists, engaged in a process of making our myth. Engaging or hacking with or co-axing with images and objects, we—the artist/character/reader—enter a new realm and sense new, unfamiliar depths of being. We become aware of things so and not so, seen and unseen, words heard and echoed. We are ushered into a third mythopoetic moment of con-fusion. We see more, deeper, sensing the dark as a place full of shadow, alive without our bidding; we hear more, deeper. In that place, to use Beckett's pun, all is "extra-audenary" (D, 293).[3] Beckett's mythopoetics offers, thus, an art form that connects art with sensory life. Born from the negative, it is nonrational art.

Beckett prepares us for the features of nonrational art in his explication of Proust's unusual artistic temperament. The first or negative phase of art that builds an other world (by undermining this one) is described by what Beckett tells us, in *Proust*, the artist is not. As an exemplar of the eccentric artist, Proust could not abide public norms, mostly because of public ignorance of the introspective life. To contrast the artist's position with the usual or public person's, Beckett says that the artist inhabits strange inner landscapes not normally understood. "Normally," Beckett writes, "we are in the position of the tourist . . . , whose aesthetic experience consists in a series of identifications and for whom Baedeker is the end rather than the means" (P, 11). The tourist, unlike the artist, walks along surfaces, guidebook in hand to explain away strangeness. The Baedeker's function is to organize perception into habituated patterns of response, making the strange familiar through strategies of identifying and naming.

An example of such a tourist is Didi in *Waiting for Godot*, who in finding himself on a country road with no familiar landmarks attempts to "translate" its strangeness. He orients himself by constant referrals to scraps of known truths, to passages from the Old Testament, jingles from vaudeville, the bones Lucky tossed, the tree in twilight. Living by a series of safe identifications, Didi hopes to anchor happenings that threaten to put him at sea. Another example is Winnie, in *Happy Days*, who, literally stuck in the ground, presents patterns of grounding in her attachments to the "old style" and to her bag of things that help to preserve normality. The artist, however, in not following the path of the norm, sets the self apart from conventional consciousness. In discussing another exemplar of artistic eccentricity, Dante, Beckett wrote: "It could even be sustained that mediocrity in the civic or religious spheres was an important condition of [Dante's] eminence in the artistic" (PD, 14).

The opposite side of civic or public involvement by the artist is solitariness. In order to create a mythopoetic aesthetic, an artist must "accomplish the negative," to use Heidegger's phrase; that is, the artist must experience a fruitfulness of stasis or feel the void as full of possibility. By active withdrawal from society, from normality, even from friendship, the artist can focus creative energy away from literal meanings into a direction of metaphor and evocation. In *Proust*, Beckett tells us that friendship is "like upholstery or the distribution of garbage buckets. It has no spiritual significance" (46). The artist emphatically "does not deal in surfaces" and therefore "the rejection of friendship is not only reasonable, but a necessity. . . . And art is the apotheosis of solitude"(46–47). To be an artist one must "stake his whole being"; one must come "from nowhere" and claim no one as brother (HH, 2).

These expressions of the negative, while revealing a certain wrath in Beckett's critical writings of the 1930s, take on a wholly different coloration fictionally in the first part of *Molloy*. There one sees a creating process at work as Molloy shrinks into himself, in utter solitude and complete forgetting. At that moment of withdrawal, Molloy achieves negative artistry. He succumbs beautifully to depths beneath his grounding: "Yes, there were times when I forgot not only who I was, but that I was, forgot to be. Then I was no longer that sealed jar to which I owed my being so well preserved, but a wall gave way and I filled with roots and tame stems for example, stakes long since dead and ready for burning, the recess of night and the imminence of dawn" (M, 49).[4]

Forgetting, indeed, accomplishes another negative requisite of Beckett's type of artist. The forgetful artist relinquishes ego, gives up ego control over the material of the text, and thereby can begin a descent into collective being. According to Beckett, Proust, the author of *Remembrance of Things Past*, had a bad memory (P, 17). Because Proust was not focused on the details of surface events, he was not keyed into habit (18). Proust's use of "involuntary memory" (19) was at once a lessening of right-mindedness and an activating of imagining. It was a process involving the emptying of mind's known or rational contents so as to receive what consciousness would not volunteer, "the best of our many selves . . . the fine essence of a smothered divinity" (19). In Proust, Beckett found the notion of "involuntary memory" entirely compatible with his own notion of "absence" or "bare presence" of mind, which he later praised in the paintings of

Henri Hayden (HH, 2). By absenting oneself, the artist can open to the springs of being.

These comments on the importance of lessening mind and of relinquishing ego can be seen in an historical as well as a critical context. On the evening of 2 October 1935 Carl Jung delivered his third lecture at the Tavistock Clinic in London, where Samuel Beckett was a patient. Beckett had come to the clinic, according to his biographer, because of his desire to talk with Geoffrey Thompson, a psychoanalyst, about the curious manner in which his works seemed to write themselves.[5] Several years earlier, in a monologue Jung had written on Joyce, Jung had discussed the idea of the artist as unwitting mouthpiece.[6] This phenomenon formed the link Jung was making between the real nature of poetry and depth psychology. Coincidentally, in 1929 Jung's article "Psychology and Poetry" appeared in the same transition issue that ran Beckett's poem "For Future Reference."[7]

Such coincidences of history, however, are less interesting than a shared agreement between an archetypal psychologist, Jung, and a poet, Beckett. Beckett's actual experience of psychic forces bears out Jung's psychoanalytic theory of the collective unconscious. Between them—doctor and artist—there is an appreciation of an other channel for creative activity. This is a channel Jung and Beckett describe as emerging from deep recesses: from nonrational material or from the lesser mind. Properly channelled, this material source can give tremendous creative energy to the receptive, waiting artist. To describe the creative process as alive with complexes would seem to negate artistry. Yet for Jung as for Beckett artistry is not a matter of ego control; rather, it is a matter of opening to the phenomena of the collective unconscious, the material of which is greater than the mere surface events of personal daily life.

That night in 1935 Jung once again was articulating his point—"We like to believe in our will-power and in our energy and in what we can do; but when it comes to a real show-down we find that we can do it only to a certain extent, because we are hampered by those little devils the complexes."[8] It is in this context that Jung then described the strange case of the little girl who had amazing mythological dreams and whose death, Jung said, was a result of her never having been born entirely (96). This girl's psychic forces were so strong, so unchannelled, that they completely overpowered her other inner system of ego control. Clearly, the wild region of the complexes is fraught with danger. Years later, in 1957, Beckett was to refer to this little girl in All That Fall (84) and to the new mind doctor who spoke of her case.

A second moment of nonrational art occurs when the artist, confronting the complexes, encounters the contents of unconsciousness. When Beckett talks of the "new thing" art must do or the "new mythological reality" of art, he is referring to the complexes, to their livingness, and to an other, non-ego side of consciousness, where objects live in the shape of images.[9] The object because of

Samuel Beckett, 1973. Reprinted by permission of John Haynes, photographer.

its outside relation to the subject cannot be possessed by any of the tricks of ego control. It cannot be subsumed into categories or families, nor can it be lured into cause-effect patterns of rational behavior. Beckett's description in *Proust* of this moment of encountering objects couldn't be clearer: "But when the object is perceived as particular and unique and not merely the member of a family, when it appears independent of any general notion and detached from the sanity of a cause, isolated and inexplicable in the light of ignorance, then and then only may it be a source of enchantment" (11).

This idea of the isolation of the object is central for an understanding of the radical difference between Beckett's poetics and that of mainstream traditional rationalism. It is an idea Beckett was to repeat with only slight variation in 1945 when he articulated the strange beauty of Bram van Velde's painting as a presentation of isolated things "needing" to be seen.[10] Such moments of new seeing force viewers to perceive their worlds differently. Having to give up the ego's old pact with reality, where art mimes surface and the artist expresses promise, viewers of mythopoetic art must re-cognize otherness. Objects, images, mirages, dreams, hallucinations, ghosts, voices—these mantic speakings come from the soul. In order for their prophetic voices to acquire meaning, however, the viewer must let go habituated patterns of perceiving.

Encountering the object as a necessary second moment of the artistic process is a foreign notion to Westerners used to classical idealism, with its postulates of harmony and personal growth. This second mythic moment puts the artist in a totally different relation to the artwork. It makes the artist—like the viewer and the character—shaped by forces that are large, vast, and difficult. Beckett's metaphor of the tourist with guidebook in hand may not be entirely helpful in understanding his criticism of ego psychology, rational humanism, and literal reality. Others in the Western tradition (besides Jung) have spoken of the complexes as phenomena of an objective, creative, other system. Merleau-Ponty, for example, writes of an invisible world that requires creation by us if we are to experience it.[11] We must all become artists, if we are to give birth to the hidden nature within ourselves, he says. Similarly, Charles Olson, Connecticut poet, draws upon a nonhumanism that rejects subject and surface in favor of objects: "What seems to me a more valid formulation for present use is 'objectism,' a word to be taken to stand for the kind of relation of man to experience which a poet might state as the necessity of a line or a work to be as wood is, to be as clean as wood is. . . . Objectism is the getting rid of the lyrical interference of the individual as ego."[12] What such a radical aesthetic proposes is that the artist avoid appeals to ego comfort. It urges instead an appreciation of intolerable images.[13]

The shift downward into the vertical axis takes Beckett to the roots of his poetics. We do not experience being if we do not experience an objective reality that can rock us out of habit into the core of being's eddy. While the ego stonewalls us on earth, the psyche releases us into the rivers of all time. We should become more like the river and less like the rock if we are to discover being's source. Confucius, the sage with long white hair (*That Time*'s old man?), uses the metaphor of man as vessel. A person should think of him- or herself not as full, complete unto the self, but as a conduit. Emptying the self of its ego contents, one becomes a sacrificial vessel of jade. One assists a larger ceremony of the sacred realm.[14] In the Western tradition the ancient alchemists thought of the vessel in their laboratories as that which allowed the opus space to grow. Any process of material change, particularly the transforming of base lead into gold, required a container to shape and give form to the new contents. To alchemists, their role was significant only insofar as they could assist this other transforming process. When they imagined the vessel as egg-shaped, they were symbolizing the idea that alchemy, because it was birthgiving, required room for gestation.

Beckett's approach to objects should be seen, I suggest, sagely and alchemically. If the artist is a shaper of a larger, deeper process, then that artist must relate entirely differently to the personal, subjective ego. "To be an artist," Beckett has said, "is to fail, as no other dare fail" (B, 13). "Failing," interpreted alchemically, is giving up humanism so that objectism can come forth; and "daring," in Jungian terms, is allowing oneself to be shaped by being.

Encountering objective reality in such a way brings about suffering, like that of dying or giving birth. Beckett describes this suffering as a freeplay of every faculty (P, 9) when ego, losing ground, flounders. One feels assaulted by the terrifying presence of otherness. Objects, not people, become energy forces; and images, like objects, displace one's sense of security in inhabiting the earth. One is at sea.

How the artist transcribes the object of such encountering into art is not made clear in Beckett's *Proust* essay. However, in later writings, Beckett discusses objects as the things that lie behind language. The artist of words must tear the language apart, as if it were a veil, in order to get at the things, the realities, they hide (L). The artistic endeavor is not a failing, it is an unveiling.[15]

From these descriptions it appears that the second moment of a mythic poetic when objective reality is encountered contains two stages. The first stage requires an artist to surrender ego, allowing—even assisting—the assault of ego. A second stage requires an artist to rend the veils that separate things hidden from things perceived. The artist engages his or her full being with an object's or image's being. The voices that speak from it, the outside, must be listened to and looked at. One encounters with amazement, enchantment, and terror these objective contents of imagination—figures, animals, images, ghosts—because these cast one onto a different proscenium of experience than one has ever known before.

Two plays of the seventies illustrate with vividness this second encountering moment of the artist/character/viewer, a moment fraught with danger. In *Not I* Demeter's story is suggested by a character called Mouth, whose spewing provides a representation of Beckett's remark in *Proust* that "the only fertile research is excavatory" (48). A mouth, as organ of creation, draws one down, not just to words of hellish experience—the Hades of Persephone—but also to an image of hell as mouth or vagina, "a supernatural-looking orifice rather than a conventional mouth image," as actress Rosemary Pountney described it.[16] The ambiguous nature of such fertile excavation, sustained throughout the play, shocks us by its rawness (on the one hand) and by its ceaselessness (on the other hand). Billie Whitelaw, who was Mouth's first actress, recalls the physical difficulties of playing the part:

> As an actress, I had to go through certain barriers that were painful. For instance, there is no time to breathe; the rib cage is pounding and pounding, and it becomes unbearably painful; going at that speed and trying to draw tiny little breaths, I would go dizzy; I would fall over at rehearsals; my jaw felt as though it had full Army kit on. . . . These were obstacles one had to crack and break through, just as an athlete does.[17]

That Time also concerns a moment of encounter with objective reality. Its effect, however, is fundamentally different; it is not that of floundering in earthbound horror but of floating in the seas of uncertainty. Another head, disembodied like Mouth, provides a focal point for audience attention. But here the old man's face is surrounded by long, flaring white hairs that, just by their placement in space, somehow soften bewilderment. Indeed, the voices that speak to the old man from both sides of his head and from above are also part of a swirl of sound that flows rather than emits. There is a sounding here, similar to what the poet Charles Olson describes as ego washed out in its own bath.[18]

The old man of *That Time* (which in myth is *illo tempore*, the no-time of the gods) allows us to sense experience, not only to think about it. While there seems to be no comprehension whatsoever on the old man's part to show that he understands why voices modulate back and forth around him and through him, that they do is sufficient. Their coming is our letting go. It now becomes our task as viewers and listeners to let the opus proceed. Beckett offers us a moment of enchantment when objects and images come forth inside darkness, space, and language.

Beckett's critical writings about this second stage of object encounter are interestingly mystical, despite the fact that he has for so long been mistermed a nihilist or a pessimist. In *Proust*, for instance, Beckett calls the experience of encountering objects "mystical" and "extratemporal" (56), partaking of "sacred action" (56). In another review he talks of a visionary experience given by the art object. He says one feels enclosed within a darker world but able finally— and in a way like Molloy—to see: "one begins finally to see in the night. In the night which is dawn and noon and evening and night. In the night which is dawn and noon and evening of an empty sky, of an unmoving earth."[19] When the dark can enlighten, one feels and sees all infinity and eternity, like Molloy, because one is no longer operating inside the sealed jar of literalism. One sees along a sacred dimension of time which moves away from single vision to what

Owen Barfield calls "double vision," what Philip Wheelwright calls "hovering presence," or what Jung distinguishes as "unconscious expression."[20] And there, down there, in space emptied of meaning, one can come face to face with the "new thing" that a mythopoetic art presents—being born from otherness.

An other self, not to be confused with the personal self of the artist, is visionary because it is nourished by the night side of life. This is an objective, not subjective, side of self, requiring a biography of text, not of person, in which fiction, not fact, forms us. When Beckett kept insisting to his autobiographer Dierdre Bair that reminiscences of his personal life would neither "help nor hinder" an understanding of his art, he was not being ornery. He was echoing a basic distinction between psychological as opposed to visionary art, one which Jung also made by saying, "and that is also why the personal life of the artist is at most a help or a hindrance, but is never essential to his creative task."[21] The subjective, personal world of ego consciousness is like the foreground of human thinking. But the visions of artists have an earth-shattering effect. Jung says—in words hauntingly like Beckett's—they "rend the curtain that veils the cosmos" (90).

A third mythopoetic moment, when sensing—not sense—is realized, occurs throughout the Beckett canon fleetingly. Characters such as Molloy or the old man in That Time partake of brief glimpses of sensing when images seem to awaken a slumbering sensory awareness. But further evidences of the night side of life occur even more radically in Rockaby and Company, when objects become animated to take on a sensual life of their own. Such animism of objects forces one to see, then to feel, perhaps finally to believe, that the soul is not, as Platonism would have it, imprisoned in Forms perceived only by reasoning minds. Soul lies, instead, buried within specific objects—windows, fish-hooks—which call forth a deep source, although clouded from the viewer or listener. Borrowing from Proust, Beckett calls objects a trigger of "involuntary" memory (P, 19) because they "hoist" (P, 19) the deep source—an other world—one not subject to the laws of will, conscious voluntarism, or reality. The deep source that objects emprison connects the perceiver to the soul and requires him or her to think again as the child thinks: nonrationally, animistically, weakly, or involuntarily. Surely, such a weakening of mind leads to one of the myths that informs Beckett's work, the myth of the non-hero.

2   The Myth of the Non-Hero: Moran

According to the mythic heroic tradition, quests into alien regions serve an initiatory function. Mortal man undergoes dangers, becomes privy to the gods' secrets, and captures the boon. In so doing, the hero transforms his condition for himself and the rest of humanity, for in touching secret treasure he acquires hidden truth and eternal wisdom. The hero of myth, as Joseph Campbell has amply explained, is essentially a double, who combines in one body both mortal and immortal aspirations. The hero demonstrates through a thousand patterns the human urge to discover godlike secrets. Campbell's description of this mythic pattern as "one hero in two aspects" expresses a basic dualistic need of the male hero to bring back the godly boon, to live the profane life more divinely, and to become integrated with the soul.[1]

As a journey into selfhood, the heroic quest traditionally takes us to other dimensions of humanness where wild things like fantasy, imagining, and fear lie beyond the gate. It is the hero's mission to conquer these wildnesses for us so that we can grasp them for ourselves and name them; then we can translate fears or fantasies into terms that make sense. The heroic venture, as a project of taking and naming, wrests what is divinely strange and other out of its context and into ours.

Especially in the Greek tradition, the heroic quest has had a decidedly male orientation. Journeys to the wilderness have long been associated with male raids upon monsters. Odysseus and the Sirens, Theseus and the Minotaur, Heracles and the lion—all recount a pattern of mythic male venturing into wild places where challenges must, like monsters, be slain. Faust's great journey to the realm of the Mothers is an extension of this pattern, whereby the strange place of otherness becomes specified as female, and the heroic conquest of wildness is a test posed by the devil. The question such journeys raise is Does the hero have what it takes? or, more importantly, Can he take what It has? Can the male hero not only discover the secrets of the gods, but can he discover the secrets of the feminine? Can these be brought back as boons?

The anti-hero movement in modern fiction alters the image of the hero as conquerer. Richard Wright's outsider, Malcolm Lowry's drunkard, Kafka's bug,

Gunter Grass's dwarf—none of these is made in the image of the traditional hero, none of these is physically attractive or strong. Yet, because he is so different, the modern anti-hero reflects an other side of the heroic impulse. For these modern types, heroism is evidenced more by willed strength than by armed response. Dr. Rieux of Camus' *The Plague* is such an anti-hero. His battle is with a monster disease, the plague, that fills the bodies of rats and men alike and defeats them. It becomes a disease of metaphysical as well as physical proportion that invades the spirit and the body and is without hope of cure. It seems to inhabit territories of being against which all human endeavor, even medical science, is helpless. However, the anti-hero can combat such an enemy with attitude. Camus invokes, as a metaphor of anti-heroism, Sisyphus, whose strength is a godlike will, a strength of mind; he has the ability to rise above torment, to live in spite of odds, to see clearly, to understand limits, and not to aspire to more.[2]

Given this tradition of heroic and anti-heroic conquest by body or by mind, the wilderness territory least explored and most feared is perhaps the only remaining frontier of modern experience—our own psychic darknesses. Conrad's quest into the "heart of darkness" is an exercise in laying bare the conditions of evil that cannot be understood by known truths nor explained by noble words. Still, Conrad's work is traditionally romantic, since he relies upon description to explore the fantastic and on narration to explain it. Then there is Marlow (Conrad's narrator), who, although humbled rather than strengthened by his wilderness experience, is still a hero—a Buddha even—because of his quest.

Beckett, however, denies us all such heroics. While his work clearly echoes heroic quest patterns, he refuses to grant us the luxury which hero patterns afford. His characters do not shoulder our burdens nor clarify our condition. They are absolutely incapable of doing so. Beckett's characters not only live inside wilderness, they are wilderness. As such, they can neither be heroic nor anti-heroic; they merely live in the dark. The questers of Beckett's fiction— those Irish "M" men Murphy, Molloy, Moran, Malone as well as the unnamed "I" characters in *Stories & Texts for Nothing* and *The Unnamable*—do not bring boon. For Beckett, the day of the hero who can help us learn the secrets or translate life's messes has passed.[3] We can expect no authority, no hero, no god, no system to throw light upon our lives. Rather, what we can expect is an un-manning of the hero. Beckett's quest by male questers begins a far more difficult task for modern consciousness—the task of undoing the ego in an attempt to rediscover the soul, or psyche. In this spirit of non-heroism, I will consider Beckett's *Molloy* in his *Three Novels*.

Many systems of meaning have been imposed upon *Molloy*, two of which deserve special mention. The first system concerns the notion of character as hero and can be seen in the approach Edith Kern took to Beckett's work over twenty years ago. She became one of the first commentators to connect *Molloy* specifically with the hero myth and with the place heroism generally takes in the stage of Western imagination. Kern contends that the two parts of *Molloy* should be reversed to be understood. By placing the second section of *Molloy* in front of the first and then reading the text through, the reader would discern an authorial purpose; that is, the reader could see clearly a pattern of the questing hero Moran searching in the depths of Molloy country for reunion with his mirrored, dark side.[4] In such a way, however, Kern makes Moran a hero of traditional quest patterns, who searches alien land for treasured boon. His quest will not only clarify his condition; it will place him once again at the center of an interpreted world.

A second system of meaning can be seen in the use of the term "metafiction" (stories within stories) to describe Beckett's challenge to the notion of authority. This challenge has been taken seriously by critics of literary theory (deconstructionists, among others) to suggest that Beckett's writing is about writing, what Robert Scholes refers to as "the possibilities and impossibilities of fiction itself."[5] Since the author, in this case Samuel Beckett, relinquishes authorial tone, using his authority only in parody, he undermines that fixed point of view which in narrative tradition has for so long been the sole, single source of irony, characterization, and structure. H. Porter Abbott proposes that Beckett's mirror effect, essentially a metafictional device, suggests a two-part repetitive structure of the Beckettian world.[6] In such a world, every fact must be repeated or sounded again, since no single incident or character can, alone, explain or expose any other single referent. Metafiction, in a sense, deconstructs the hero myth of the centered search. Inger Christensen suggests that Beckett's style serves the purpose of defeating the notion of character as hero through such means as anonymity of name, brevity of speech, audience aside, and immobility of movement.[7] And as early as 1971 David Hesla raised a similar point when he described Beckett's chaos by means of the shape of the parabola. Moran in *Molloy* becomes for Hesla "a parabolic presentation of a certain facet of the task of writing," no one point any more meaningful or central than any other point, since all points are equidistant from the fixed line of narration.[8]

Moran's quest indeed does mirror Molloy's and, through this mirroring strategy, does achieve an important negation. As James Eliopolos implies in his critique there is an emphasis within this negation away from character-as-hero toward language-as-hero. In its ability to mirror, to repeat, to circle back on itself, language assumes center stage, taking over the place that the hero had traditionally occupied. But language does so, Eliopolos asserts, in a strangely heroic way. For in its ability to repeat constantly and maddeningly, language provides a power of its own to destroy as well as to create the very thoughts that it first sets down.[9]

My suggestion, however, is that Beckett's *Molloy* actually accomplishes a different kind of negation, the purpose of which is to weaken the heroic concept, together with its accompanying pose of author's authority, language literalism, and ego superiority. Patterns of repetition, contradiction, and regression undermine the heroic stance until the hero is brought—quite literally—to his knees. This new non-hero of Beckett's world places us at the center of confusion— along with the artist and the characters. In this dramatic process Beckett decenters the heroic male ego, as Moran, in the second section of *Molloy*, illustrates so well. The hero as two-in-one becomes not a means of elevating the male human hero toward his godlike capabilities, but rather a means of initiating him into psychic awareness. As I shall discuss, Moran's journey is fundamentally regressive, taking him back to where soul—not ego—lives.

Beckett prepares us for a subversion of the hero as a god, twinned with the supernatural, when he portrays Moran as mock patriarch and a mock hunter. Moran's ridiculous sense of ownership seeks to turn his garden into a fort and the wilderness into his kingdom. He talks boastfully of "my little garden," "my lemon verbena," "my turkey," and "my daisies" (M, 93). Only a matter of degree separates these comforts from the other pile of possessions Moran adds to his hoard, including "my beloved church" and "my son." When Gaber (the angel Gabriel?) visits Moran in the garden that Sunday, bearing word from Youdi (Yahweh?), we as readers are being set up for a heroic tale of salvation and transformation. Moran encourages our delusion about his heroics by his insufferably paternalistic stance toward "his" son and by his ridiculous obedience toward "his" church. His need to take communion before embarking on his mission is more a need to impress Father Ambrose than a desire to repent or receive. Clearly, we are in an Old Testament world of monotheism, where Moran thinks "in monologue" (95) and worships commandment.

As non-hero, Moran is also non-hunter. On the literal level he is a paid agent whose job at this time is to hunt down Molloy. He dresses for the venture like a country sportsman, selecting his pepper-and-salt shooting-suit, complete with knee-breeches and black shiny boots (M, 124). To his hat he attaches a string, a signal that he is a fox hunter or a gentleman of sport.[10] The stick, which enables sharper contact with the prey, and a "massive-handled winter umbrella" (124) are, together, like a sickle that can cut down any enemy, ward off any hazard.

Now for Beckett's characters, the sickle emblem—crutch, stick, umbrella—is both an instrument of destruction and of intellection. Its many occurrences in both the fiction and the plays attest to its symbolic connection with the old man figure, the old hero, and the old ego. The unknown speaker in *The Unnamable*, for instance, relates a tale of his journey home on crutches which he sinks into the entrails of his mother (U, 323–24), and blind Hamm in *Endgame* depends on his gaff to help him interpret the surfaces of his world. Moran's sickle emblem recalls the mythical old king Cronus, a remote and terrible ruler who castrated his father with a sickle and swallowed his children. The sickle, tool of power, is Cronus's means of maintaining order as sky god and enacting the role of the abominated father. There is, however, another side to Cronus's character, which is associated with a very different function—not as father-king, dark and tyrannical ruler, but as harvester, gentle son of mother earth. The sickle in the second instance is an implement for reaping grain or tall grass. Thus, the sickle is literally a two-edged sword that cuts both ways. The fact that it has taken on such strongly negative connotations when seen with Cronus suggests the degree to which the old king has severed himself from his roots with Gaea. But it also suggests the intriguing possibility that lies within this figure to transform himself, to become other than he appears.

Indeed, Beckett's Moran is a type of Cronus, a literal two-face, whose pose of godliness is but the thinnest disguise, even to himself. We see this double-edged susceptibility of Moran's in two quite different ways. On the one side, he betrays an openness to harvesting the fields of imagination. He shows true affinity with Molloy, that creature of the wilds, when, just before his son abandons him, he finds himself in the middle of a fold of sheep and seems to merge with their movements: "Yes, little by little, one by one, they turned and faced me, watching me as I came. Here and there faint movements of recoil, a tiny foot stamping the ground, betrayed their uneasiness. . . . And I was wondering how to depart without self-loathing or sadness, or with as little as possible, when a kind of immense sigh all round announced it was not I who was departing, but the flock" (M, 158, 159). Here is Moran catching the eyes of sheep as Molloy had caught the eyes of donkeys (M, 26), Moran remembering his roots in mother earth. The other, more pronounced side of Moran, however, is his moronic insistence on will. In his will to rule, to lord over, to decree, Moran betrays a chronic danger of heroes who forget their roots and rack their brains.

Jung spoke of this point in his third Tavistock lecture. He was referring to a patient whom he found overly secure in the head. The patient had had a dream which Jung said gave a clear picture, through the dreamer's image of the magic wand, of the fortressed ego. The wand, Jung said, is an instrument, and "instruments in dreams mean what they actually are, the devices of man to concretize his will. . . . An instrument is a mechanism which represents my will, my intelligence, my capability and my cunning. . . . What does this mean? It means that [the dreamer] simply thinks that the danger does not exist. . . . That is how people behave who consist of the head only. They use their intellect in order to think things away; they reason them away."[11] Similarly, Moran's sickle-like stick, his pointed umbrella, and his fondness of hard sounds like the clicking of a mallet or a rake through pebbles (M, 93): these concretions inspire the mind to work sharply. Moran's comment on the evening of his departure is typical of a mind too full of itself: "and birds of course, blackbird and thrush, their song sadly dying, vanquished by the heat, and leaving dawn's high boughs for the bushes' gloom" (93). His fondness for sky creatures and lofty turns of phrase needs to be grounded, brought back and down, reconnected with the world of senses.

The situation in which we find Moran in the second half of the novel thus sets up a counterpart to the situation in the first half, tying the novel together as two halves of a still incomplete whole. Immured in social concerns and external biddings, Moran has lost his center, having given it over to ego. Metaphorically, Moran has lost Molloy, the mother's son that he once was. That he has to hunt for Molloy like quarry or prey is just another indication of how far removed he is from selfhood and how far down he must go to recover psychic depth.

Soon enough, Moran's mission becomes a quest, where will, intellect, and purpose weaken, and where the process of reconnecting with the soul begins. The first weakening occurs when Moran is in the bathroom giving an enema to his son. There, surrounded by porcelain, hard, white objects, and chromium, Moran takes control of his son's anal condition as if it were a hunter's moment. His son, literally beneath him, gives him the feeling of superiority, of being able to "score" a hunter's hit (M, 119). He feels himself "at peace" as he wages this war. Moran plays little games to outfox his son, knowing, with the cunning of Cronus, that unless he set traps for the child, the child will set traps for him.

Moran's interpreted world, however, is suddenly broken into when he experiences a sharp pain in his knee. Ultimately, it is the knee that brings him to his senses—literally as well as figuratively. By having to lean on a crutch, not just use it as a sickle, and having to lean on his child, not just use him as a whipping board, Moran forms a new relationship with the grounds of being. Also, by having to experience language, not just use it rhetorically, his propensity for literalness softens until figures of speech—like "on one's knees" or "out of joint"—become living metaphors.

Of course, Moran is already a weakened character in the reader's eye by virtue of his similarity with Molloy, from the novel's first section—Molloy, bound to horizons, bound to earth, bound to mother. Like Moran, Molloy is a man with a stick or a man who talks about a man with a stick (M, 16, 18), each character putting one in mind of the other. But unlike Moran, Molloy, whose name ends in vowels not consonants, understands earth rather than sky. He feels tied figuratively to the animals of earth—sheep, goats, donkeys, dogs—and talks about the several figurative windows in his head which look out and frame for him those parts of the universe which he can never hope to know (51). Beckett's use of repetition within the two parts of the novel suggest further ways in which Moran and Molloy, as opposites, are meant to come together. Both lie down on the ground (69, 201); both leave through a wicket gate (70, 74); both describe their own bicycle as having a "buckled" wheel (88, 215). But the additional fact that each man leans on crutches as mode of locomotion establishes an even more important condition of their connection through weakening. For it is the crutch that forces communication between head and foot, between what one wills to do with the mind and what one cannot will in the body, between ego and psyche. It is the crutch that, like a sickle, connects the opposites.

Three moments, then, characterize the unmaking of the hero concept and the weakening of egoistic will: the moments of regressing, encountering, and sensing. Seen early in Beckett's career, as here in the trilogy, these moments have remained constant mythic themes throughout his writing. Because of Beckett's intent to undo the hero construct in fiction, in poetry, in drama—as well as in a psychology of egoism and rationalism—and because this intent has been with him for so long, its early expression deserves close examination.

Regressing, as I have said, is the initial physical weakening of Moran's bodied, literal strength. Beckett gives the idea of being brought "to the knees" metaphoric reality, as we see just how humbling a posture it is to be brought down. Moran, on his knees, is lowered, taken down against his will, made to feel mud and root—how it is to be "literally uprooting" (M, 165). Uprooted, Moran becomes his own metaphor when he grovels with his head close to the roots of earth. Metaphor acquires a literal sense and the literal takes on metaphoric reality. Moran's instruction by his boss Youdi to write a report, thus, is impossible after such an experience, for the logic demanded of report writing is Cronus-logic, the chronology of literal doings. But Moran's doings have turned that logic inside out and upside down. His feeble joke indicates that the life that runs out of him—"I knew not through what breach" (102)—is the old life of outer garbs (like the breeches of his sporting costume) which become "breaches" or juncture places for backwards birth. [12]

Moran's regressing is suggested through another image in the text—child as leader of the way. Moran, impaired at the knee, unable to walk upright, must depend as never before on his son Jacques, whom he has forbidden to get ahead of him. By the child's leadership the pair is taken into a childlike region that totally defies Moran's will. Through the wicket gate, down the left path, the two take a journey that recalls Virgil, whose Dantean journey limping through hell toward paradise is a matter of seeking the left path of intuition, not the right path of will. [13] The quest is difficult, for it puts one on a different footing with the unknown. Moran tries to focus his mind in its usual beaconlike deductiveness, but a voice, speaking as a child with a babble of sound, begins prompting his thought. "Unfathomable mind," Moran says, "now beacon, now sea" (M, 106). The whole scene assumes fantastical proportion when Moran's words get hopelessly confused by a repetition of ba-ba syllables: "we have another system, of singular beauty and simplicity, which consists of saying Bally (since we are talking of Bally) when you mean Bally and Ballyba when you mean Bally plus its domains exclusive of Bally itself. I myself for example lived, and come to think of it still live, in Turdy, hub of Turdyba" (134).

Subsequently, Moran's mindfulness becomes more and more childlike. He shows a new willingness to surrender to the "spray of phenomena" (M, 111) in the world outside his garden, allowing, as a child might, his senses not his will to guide him. He listens, now, to birds—not with an ear to catch the right rhetorical turn for his phrase but with a surrender to their sounds (145). Weakening to the child's world of sounds is thus fundamentally a return to Molloy's depth. With new poetic listening, Moran turns backwards to hear the silence (145), to listen to his knee (147), to merge with the little sighing movements of sheep and dogs (159), and to return to the flies (166).

The non-hero's first moment of regression takes literal phrases, turns them, and turns them again, until their literal meanings and forward thrusts of narration must stop. For the old hero construct, the old ego, the old king Cronus, or the old man figure like Moran, such turns in phraseology are little black pauses where metaphors can be harvested. Metaphors can be seen anew— not as literal embellishments of meaning—but as figures to be reckoned with. This is a process of the psyche coming alive and of the will losing its way (M, 131).

A second moment in the unmaking or regressing of the hero occurs when the backwards direction of the quest takes the quester into confrontation with the beasts he refuses to acknowledge because they have been swallowed or repressed. Associated earlier with upright posture, birds, and bombast, Moran now begins to be associated with a lower species, particularly with dogs. All this is in preparation for an encountering moment with his own beast that "dogs" him. He comments, for instance, on his fondness of his dog Zulu; he sees a dog in Molloy country (M, 153); he feels the eyes of a dog upon him (159); he is dogged by his own shadow; he says he is out in weather not fit for a dog (173); he is treated like a dog; and he lives a dog's life. There is even the strange image of Moran and his son tied together, like two dogs on a leash (129). In becoming the figures of his own speech, Moran begins to harvest their meaning, actually and literally confronting them, not as constructs of his mind (ego) but as realities of imagination (psyche).

This point is seen in the encountering moment when Moran's journey backwards forces him into battle with his other side, the beast of his own literalisms—Molloy. Because Moran's connections with the child and the dog have achieved a weakening of his heroic stance, we are prepared for failed battle. What we can expect and what does happen is negative accomplishment, whereby a weakened hero succumbs to his monster. In such a manner, Moran becomes twinned with earth not sky, turns back to a place where opposites combine, and seeks the mother. Moran thus sets in motion the non-hero pattern of Beckett's work.

Moran's battle with the beast has all the overtones of myth but without the usual mythic conclusions. As with all mythic moments, the battle with the beast takes place by the waters of transformation. In like fashion, Moran drags himself to a stream, out in the middle of the wilderness and sees—most unexpectantly—his quarry. It is the moment he has been waiting for. But rather than recalling such heroic wrestlings of, say, Hercules with the Nemean lion, this encounter recalls a much different myth. It recalls Narcissus, the hunter, who looks into the pool of reflection and sees Echo, that is, the other self. It is a moment of ego forgetting and self or soul remembering. Narcissus and Moran are both hunters on target, but when they gaze into the waters of transformation they become dislocated and dispossessed. Moran describes the encountering moment as follows:

> I saw a man a few paces off, standing motionless. He had his back to me. He wore a coat much too heavy for the time of the year and was leaning on a stick so massive, and so much thicker at the bottom than at the top, that it seemed more like a club. He turned and we looked at each other for some time in silence. . . . There was a coldness in his stare. . . . He had a huge shock of dirty snow-white hair. I had time, before he squeezed it back in under his hat, to see the way it swelled up on his skull. . . . He made a curious movement, like a hen that puffs its feathers and slowly dwindles till it is smaller than before. (M, 145–46)

Here in the image Molloy presents to Moran, we see the familiar Cronus features of old man, old king, Old Testament God. The coldness, the white hair, the sickle-like instrument—all are there. Molloy, as Moran's echo, allows Moran to get a glimpse of who he, Moran, is. But what a strange thing it is—for the image harbors within itself both ambivalence and paradox. The figure is huge and birdlike, massive and delicate. It has an immense skull, suggesting an enormous ability to think and talk; but it communicates dumbly, by gesture only. The overall effect of this beast, so lumbering and yet so henlike, is to throw Moran out of his mindset. When the figure appears again (M, 149) its second appearance—far from clarifying the first—only complicates it. The face, now in better focus, is full of wounds. When the figure appears a third time it reveals a terrible truth to Moran, with its ferrety eyes and mouth reddened from trying to "shit its tongue" (151). Moran observes in the figure something of his own brutal nature, which surfaces in a literal form as the brute before him. When Moran grapples with, then beats the brute to death, he has not simply accomplished his mission to kill Molloy. He has, on a deeper level, killed off his own, inner beast—the monster side of himself that literalizes events, tyrannizes children, and stonewalls the ego.

In the third book of the trilogy (*The Unnamable*) of which *Molloy* is the first, Beckett shows that the beast of egoism is a thing petrified by its own literalism. "I have always been sitting here, at this selfsame spot, my hands on my knees, gazing before me like a great horn-owl in an aviary. The tears stream down my cheeks from my unblinking eyes" (U, 293). This figure has been on the outpost of humanity for so long that its tears and the stone of its face blend into one. Its sadness has a coldness in it like that of Cronus or Saturn. Yet, oddly, its heaviness attracts, like a magnet, bringing into focus an other which comes out of nowhere and moves like a mirage. Beckett's description of the Unnamable and his overladen ego follows: "The other advances full upon me. He emerges as from heavy hangings, advances a few steps, looks at me, then backs away. He is stooping and seems to be dragging invisible burdens. What I see best is his hat. The crown is all worn through, like the sole of an old boot" (298).

Here, in *The Unnamable*, the old king Cronus figure is drawn more explicitly than in the other two parts of *Three Novels*. In this strange figure we meet many other old king figures, not only Moran, but also Hamm in *Endgame*, and Pozzo in *Waiting for Godot*, and Henry in *Embers*; all of whom are stooped by burdens and wear hollow crowns. From this stoney figure (at the end of the trilogy) to the picture of Moran (at the beginning) sitting on a milestone in the dark, "eyes fixed on the earth as on a chessboard" (M, 125), the quest has taken us backwards. One image reminds us of an earlier image, just as one repetition echoes another. By meeting the beast and murdering it, Moran becomes Molloy who, like the Unnamable, becomes real in the way archetypes are real. [14]

At the end of the Molloy section Moran's beastly ego has been slain. He is not the composed unit he once was; his face, like Molloy's, now contains deep lesions (M, 170). Dragging himself flat on his belly back to an abandoned home, he is lessened. Thus, while Moran has accomplished his mission, he has only just begun his quest. What emerges is the half-truth of poetry, where truths exist side by side: "It is midnight. . . . It was not midnight" (176). Such poetic truths are factual lies to the literal mind. For the literalist, things cannot be so and not so at the same time. But for the non-hero, who lives the lie of poetry, contradiction describes reality. When Beckett leaves the reader listening to contradictory statements at the end of *Molloy*, he is inviting the reader to embark upon a different quest—a journey into psychic depth.

3   The Old Man and Echo

Ovid's telling of the myth of Narcissus is a story concerned with a change in the very nature of things.[1] According to Ovid, Narcissus was a beautiful hunter boy who had a pride so great that he could be touched by no one, neither boy nor maid. The nymph Echo, seeing Narcissus out in the country, burned with desire for him; however, because she had been punished, she could not talk to him directly about her love. When she called, she heard only her own echo, and he heard only a voice in the wilderness. Unable to reach Narcissus, Echo pined away: her body shriveled, her bones turned to stone, and her voice was all that remained.

In the second part of the tale, the fate of Narcissus acts as a counterpart to that of Echo—an echo of Echo. One day Narcissus went to the bottom of the wood where he hoped to satisfy his deep thirst in the still waters of a shaded pool. Leaning to drink, he saw in the water an image. So taken was he by the reflection that he developed a passion for it. Like Echo, his suffering is his undoing; the fires of thirst, his unbecoming; and like her, his flesh falls to the greensward.

Beckettian motifs resound in this tale, particularly in Ovid's version of it. One notes, for instance, a familiar division into twos: a tension between extremes in nature (fire and water) and extremes in character (passion and yearning); between nature's metamorphosis of character (bones into stone) and character's metamorphosis of nature (water into tears). One notes too, in Ovid as in Beckett, a tension between the essence of being and the essence of feeling. Suffering as a tensive part of being is essentially poetic. When one hears pain as alliterative, rhythmic, full of consonant and vowel patterns, full of beat, one is hearing Echo. In these depths, there is beauty.[2]

At least two of Beckett's critics have remarked on a Beckettian connection with Narcissus. Jean-Jacques Mayoux has commented that Ovid's mythic telling "will be with Beckett as long as he lives [and] might serve as the general title of his opus."[3] Lawrence Harvey has observed that the myth brings out "man's complex relationship to the other" in terms of "man's need to possess what is other, or to give himself to the other."[4] These comments set the story of Narcissus as a paradigm for Beckett's themes, images, and language patterns. But, by focussing

Roman tragic mask of the first–second century A.D., formerly of the Townley Collection. Photograph reproduced by courtesy of the Trustees of the British Museum.

on Echo rather than Narcissus, it is my intention to show that sight, sound, and feel are the touchstones that lead narcissistic old men down to layers of undiscovered being.

The myth of Narcissus first makes its appearance in Beckett's work with an early collection of poems entitled *Echo's Bones*. These thirteen poems are distinguished by their complex use of idiom and image, by a certain bitterness of tone, and by a specific quality which generally marks the writings of Beckett at this early period—a deliberate desire to confound. The reader familiar with Beckett's later works, however, is struck by the way this small collection brings out images and themes that, forty and fifty years later, have acquired fathoms of meaning. Tales of love are told in this collection by an old man, worn out and sterile. And yet they contain an undeniable link to the myth which centers them, as if the work itself, Beckett's corpus, offers itself as a reflecting pool for readers.

References in the poems to open fields and pagan lands, for instance, suggest that the quest of the narcissistic hunter—the old man of Beckett decked out in boots and suit, hat and coat—must take him from peaks of ego to vales of soul. In "Eneug I" the old man figure moves from the "bush of gorse on fire in the mountain" down into the "sunk field" with "mushy toadstool" (EB, 24), oozing and soaking up the sky. In "Sanies I" the old man's wanderings take him up hill and down dale where he becomes distraught by fauns and nymphs (31). In "Malacoda" the old man's quest takes him to the edge of water and to an implied death, after he has been immersed "knee deep" in garden weeds (43–44).

This hunterly quest downwards and backwards initiates the old man into his echoes. It is the moment of encountering, the second moment of mythic journeying, when the hunter-traveller must pause in one particular space, that void; it is the moment when senses can come forth. Echoes resound in the poems when the old man sees colors that are not just any colors, and flowers that are not just any flowers. In "Serena II" the "xanthic flowers" (38) the ferns, and the asphodels (39)—not just any flowers—recall the flowers of the mythic underworld. In the quest to dis-cover, one really un-covers, then re-covers and re-members, putting back together hidden truths. Although the old man in this cycle of thirteen poems sets out to seek only himself (in the clonal earth that "Serena II" images [38]), cloning is not the answer and does not satisfy the thirst. For underneath all surfaces lies an other world, different rather than clonal. This other world is full of resonance, in which Echo will sound out.

But to appreciate these great inward metamorphoses, as Moran put it (M, 163), we have to see Beckett's narcissists alone in their solitary condition. Moran, of course, is one of Beckett's early fictional representatives of solitary senility, as chapter 2 has described. Murphy is another. As Beckett's first narcissist, Murphy exemplifies the absurdity of desiring to be cloned in the image of oneself, shut off from all echo. His is a life of inaction (Mur, 38): passivity raised to an art. Murphy is "addicted" to the dark (26) and to "remaining still for long periods" (27). His is a "passion" for "the trussed condition" (30)—pun and irony intended. He thinks he can replicate joy in his solitary life by tying his body into a rocking chair with scarves so as to rock his mind out of the land of the living into the land of the dead. His need to disconnect his mind actually from all-that-is reflects a desire to return to stasis. And his peculiar eating habits, "the same as always" (96), together with the picture he has of his mind, "a large hollow sphere, hermetically closed to the universe without" (107), reflect his desire for extreme stability. Indeed, Murphy's fundamental purpose in life— to seek "the torpor he had been craving" (105)—reflects Narcissus's desire to center the self in literalism rather than image, in body rather than psyche, in ego rather than soul.

The word "narcissus" comes from the Greek narkē, meaning "torpor; all that is useless."[5] Encapsulated inside an echoless ego, the narcissist languishes and goes nowhere, until stasis becomes a kind of death. Again Beckett recalls Narcissus when Murphy sees himself in Mr. Endon (a psychotic patient in an asylum), who sees no one but himself, each a clone of the other. Mr. Endon, we are told, is "all languor," "immune." He has a psychosis "so limpid and imperturbable that Murphy felt drawn to it as Narcissus to his fountain" (Mur, 186).

This disconnection from the roots of self is realized most forcefully when Murphy attempts to actually "be" Mr. Endon, literalizing Mr. Endon's condition for himself. It is a moment reminiscent of Narcissus. Murphy flings himself down to the ground in an effort to bring forth images: of his mother, of his father, of Celia (his mistress), of the whole crowd of Murphy characters: and, finally, of images of other characters, like Bim from How It Is (Mur, 251). But Murphy's attempts to will such images of the past—to literalize them by an effort of the rational, thinking mind—fails utterly. Mind at work with itself, alone, is like a king that rules with a hollow crown. Even in these early works of Beckett, Echo undermines the narcissist, who needs to rediscover sensing through imaging.

Another specific reference to the Narcissus myth occurs in Molloy, written almost twenty years after Murphy. Moran, leaving the peaks of his security systems, has ventured into the wilderness with his child. On his own, since his son Jacques has gone off in search of a bicycle, Moran "surrenders" himself to nature's sounds and sights, hearing them "borne" to him "on the air" (M, 145). "Born" backwards into wonders of sensing, Moran finds his other Molloy self in images that clearly imply Narcissus: "I dragged myself down to the stream. I lay down and looked at my reflection, then I washed my face and hands. I waited for my image to come back, I watched it as it trembled towards an ever increasing likeness" (145). After this visual encounter between Moran and his echo self, Molloy, there are two tactile encounters prior to the killing described in chapter

2. First, Moran and Molloy touch fingers and exchange hands on the stick (146), Moran's hand under Molloy's.[6] Then Molloy "throws" a last look at Moran, as if a look can be "caught" or "grasped" by hands. These actions literalize metaphors of the senses; they make metaphors real, giving metaphor not just a literary quality but an actuality in sensory experience. Moran, now ready to kill his beastly self, resurrects Echo.

The importance of metaphoric as opposed to literal reality is key to a Jungian approach to soul, or self, rather than a Freudian approach to ego. It separates, as well, a metaphoric as opposed to a literal reading of the myth of Narcissus. Murray Stein, a Jungian psychoanalyst, discusses the mythic moment of seeing one's face, as Narcissus does in the waters of the woods, as an occasion for self-reflection. He says, "the reflection back of an image of the subject . . . is a genuine reflection of his own unconscious face. . . . Thus the vision of himself that he finds in the eyes of his beloved can become the occasion for self-reflection."[7] Similarly, Gaston Bachelard, in one of his several phenomenological writings on the four elements of nature, muses on water's function for Narcissus at the edge of the bank. What, Bachelard wonders, is water metaphorically, and what is the connection between water and soul? In his L'eau et les rêves, Bachelard speaks to this point: "la fountain est pour lui [Narcissus] un chemin ouvert" (the fountain is for him [Narcissus] an open way).[8] What these metaphorical musings suggest is that there is an aspect of Narcissus which needs to be looked at differently, poetically, if we are to gain insight into how ego loses itself in reverie. For there, at water's edge, a way "opens" (Bachelard) or an "occasion" presents itself (Stein). Such an "occasional way" formulates a central poetic image of Beckett's writing.

We hear echoes of Beckett's old man at the water's edge in two radio plays, Embers and Cascando and in the BBC production of Endgame. In the latter play, Hamm (like Henry in Embers) feels a dripping in his head. Choosing to interpret the dripping sound as "an inexorable insistence of a metronome, with an echo effect added," the BBC production was drawing listeners' attention to what is often overlooked in Hamm's stage character; namely, that Hamm's head is really a cavern with leaks in it.[9] In forcing us to sense our literal world differently, Beckett's senescent male narcissists urge us, as readers and listeners, ever deeper into Echo's cave.

So, too, are we drawn to the characters through sound in the plays for radio, and so are the characters drawn into our minds through sound. The effect this has on us is unsettling; for, while we expect plot to be charted in a forward movement of time, we are disappointed at every turn. The plot direction goes only backwards, where sounds speak, urging us to reconsider, regroup, remember. These speakings, however, are the voices of Echo, who opens old egos to "occasions" for self-reflection.

Is it any wonder, then, that water plays such an important part in Beckett's early radio plays? The old man's still waters of consciousness need roiling. In his chronically profane earth-boundedness, the old man has sought to root out connection, to avoid memory, to slam the door on pain. And yet, for all his egocentrism, Beckett's old man narcissist is pained, does suffer, and feels loss. But the feelings have no words for their expression, since words have lost their sensory connectedness with music. What the old man needs, Beckett shows us, is a new sounding and a new flow, where Echo can come forth.

Embers, as a title, suggests the following point: that small burning coals of selfhood lie buried, waiting to be warmed into newness, that is, to be said differently, "uttered" anew. This is true of Henry who—never having been able to leave the firey hell of his father's rejection—has never been able to rise from the literalness of his father's words: "A washout, that's all you are, a washout!" (Emb, 102). Henry's father, having described his son negatively in terms of water, literalizes his own metaphor by drowning himself. This death by water etches itself like fire into the son's memory. Talking to his now-dead father, Henry says, "you wanted the sun on the water for that evening bathe you took once too often . . . (*Pause.*) We never found your body, you know" (96). Beckett's use of the word "sun" complicates the word "son," suggesting that a father's love for his son is like a setting sun—deathly—but also that a son must walk on water, Christ-like, if he is to earn his father's love or save his father from doing deadly deeds.

Yet precisely because of such despair, Henry—or any son—can rise again. Beckett's sea sounds suggest that when Henry obsessively retraces his own steps to the sea in an effort to understand his father's suicide, Henry is also resurrecting the powers of imagination. As the play's sounds imply, the sea moves variously: now dripping and leaky, now calm, now roaring. The tides of the sea resist external control. Henry's is a life controlled by non-sea sounds: the baton of his daughter's music master, the hoof beats of a horse, his own retracing of his own father's steps. But by seeking closeness with the sea's rhythm, Henry can attempt to vary the rhythm of his own literal turn of mind. Perhaps then he can realize that water—the major symbol of his father's death and the major metaphor of his father's rejection of him—can shift its literal harshness in his mind. Perhaps the tides of the sea can wash out the literal ego that seeks to drown the soul.

In *Embers*, then, the sea takes on the quality of Echo as a living character both in background and metaphor. Beckett's stage directions make this backgrounding explicit: *"Scarcely audible"* in the beginning, the sea is *"still faint, audible throughout what follows whenever pause indicated"* (95). The sea fills the gaps of all silence, to be heard as a constant amidst the many fluctuations of time and memory. To Ada, Henry's wife, the sea is lovely and soothing, "like another time, in the same place" (106). For her the earth, full of holes, opens (113). Her femaleness allows her to experience constant little places of rebirth in nature through the gaps in her life. But Henry's experience is the opposite. For him the sea is a vulture woman with lips and claws. "Listen to it! (*Pause.*) Lips and claws! (*Pause.*) Get away from it! Where it couldn't get at me!" (106). Each time he approaches the sea's edge on the "deeply shelving beach" (111), Henry delves deeper into the sea's depths, also into the origins of his own despair. When, finally, he describes himself (as Bolton) in his story, he is at a low ebb of feeling. But because he is so far down, he is closer than he has ever been to an imaginal turning point.

Henry's story is a tale of two old men, Bolton and Holloway, standing before a fire on a cold winter's night. Bolton is in great distress and has summoned Holloway to come help him. When Bolton suddenly lights a candle and looks Holloway deep in the eye, he sees, in effect, an echo of himself and the hollowness of his way. For the eye mirrored back to him is old: "the old blue eye, very glassy, lids worn thin, lashes gone, whole thing swimming, and the candle shaking over his head" (Emb, 120). Holloway's eye thus expresses an ambivalence of the central water metaphor of the play. Peculiarly without depth or feeling, the eye reflects empty insight: it is like a dead sea, with its lashes gone and sense of nonreflection. But it also reflects an open "way" for soul and an "occasion" for grief, since Holloway's eye swims in tears.

As the archetypal old man, however, Henry fights against the ambivalence of story's metaphor, seeking only to keep his life in a forward direction, away from the painful past. Henry's need to keep out the double valences of meaning is further echoed in the passages concerned with the music master (another Henry figure) who, slamming his ruler on the piano at Henry's daughter, is fighting to make the eff sound pure (Emb, 107–8). This fierce anger of the music master mirrors Henry's own fear of what threatens to break through the thuds: "(*wildly.*) Thuds, I want thuds! Like this! (*He fumbles in the shingle, catches up two big stones and starts dashing them together.*) Stone! (*Clash.*) Stone! (*Clash . . .*)" That's life! (*He throws the other stone away. Sound of its fall.*) Not this . . . (*pause*) . . . sucking!" (112–13). Henry's wildness, like the roaring of the sea, expresses his need to slam the door on life, to shut out violent eruptions. It is an urge that seeks as well to tame uncontrollable gallops of imagination. When Henry asks if a horse can "mark time" (105), he is hoping against hope that unrestrained forces—in himself, in his father before him, in the music master, in the sea—can be brought under control, so as to hold time to a metered march, not a flowing waltz.

But other stories and other characters underlie the tragic past which still rules Henry's life. These characters—Ada, Addie, Bolton, Holloway—are what Bachelard calls the *moins-êtres*, the sub-beings, who either because they are imaginary or because they are connected downward to the feminine psyche, offer possibilities (like the sea) for infinite change.[10] Of these sub-beings, the sea is the most potent in the play, acting as Echo to the old man's narcissism. So when the key tragic event of Henry's life is described in terms of a row, we hear two things. We hear "row" as the argument between father and son that presumably caused the father's suicide: "We were all shouting at one another" (Emb, 116); and we also hear it as that "row" Henry and Ada took when they were in love: "Let us go for a row" (115). Two opposite emotions—hate and love—swirl together around a single word, making that word bear more meaning. The sea also forms the key metaphor to describe Henry and his father who are "washouts" in each other's eyes: "You wouldn't know me now, you'd be sorry you ever had me, but you were that already, a washout, that's the last I heard from you, a washout" (101). Dialogue merges here into monologue; meanings swim together. Both father and son seem dead to each other. Yet both, in their anger and frustration, echo each other's metaphors: the father washes himself out to sea; the son drowns himself in tears. One wonders where is Echo's voice in the nature of these things? Where is Echo's beauty?

Jung responded to this problem of painful beauty when he wrote an astonishing piece on Joyce's *Ulysses*. At first, Jung admits to flat-out rejection of Joyce's novel on the grounds that it insults conventions of feelings, disappoints expectations for content, and destroys criteria of art. But then he meditates on his own negative reactions. He says that abusiveness springs "from the resentment of the unmodern man who does not wish to see what the gods graciously veil from his sight."[11] Like Joyce, Beckett rends the veil. Like Joyce, Beckett exposes pain. Unlike Joyce, Beckett shows pain's stark beauty again and again in his work—not to elevate our senses, but to deepen them. For Beckett, pain reveals a world full of stones with only an image to cling to. Henry, thus, clings to the image of his father alone on a stone looking out to sea; he circles around this image imaginatively in his head, telling stories. Literally, too, Henry clings to the image of his father when he walks to the edge of the sea, re-tracing his father's suicidal steps, and when he circles with his hands, grinding stones together. Henry's imaginative and literal work with personal pain is, subsequently, a creative act of first importance. By going back over the source of his pain in various modes, Henry is engaging in play: he is playing with the gap in his life, transforming it, softening it, changing it from its literalness in mere statement or mere time.

Cascando continues the themes of *Embers* and *Words and Music*, that is, of characters wrestling with sounds. Two voices, one called "Opener," "dry as dust," the other called Voice, "low" and "panting," are like elements such as earth and fire. Between them, these two elemental characters create a picture of the sea and of Woburn, the only human character, who, although "heading nowhere" (Cas, 15), slogs slowly toward the sea. Heard intermittently, sometimes alone, sometimes with one or another of the two other voices, is Music, playing airs and acting as the fourth element, air. The play reiterates familiar themes with the familiar old man character. Wearing the "same old coat" and carrying the "same old stick," this character reminds us of the Molloys and Morans of other stories who have also had to pull themselves through the dark. But underlying the sameness here is a difference of intensity—as if this outing, although not seen, can enlighten us.

This strange sense of harmony among the elements is Echo at play. Yet, another sense invoking Narcissus by the edge of the bank is disharmonious, turning Voice into a ludicrous series of lumbering falls: "the bank . . . he hugs the bank . . . same old stick . . . he goes down . . . falls . . . on purpose or not . . . can't see . . . he's down . . . that's what counts . . . face in the mud . . . arms spread . . . that's the idea" (Cas, 11). This is not a journey we can make sense of. Each time Voice tells us Woburn is "up" on his feet, he then describes him "down"—"ton weight . . . in the sand . . . knee-deep . . . he goes down" (12). The maddening inelegance of these up-but-mostly-down movements expresses something very primal about Woburn's will, as if will, a fifth element among the other four, is cut off from Voice or Opener or Music and is thwarted by the sea: "no tiller . . . no thwarts . . . no oars . . . afloat . . . sucked out . . . then back . . . aground . . . drags free . . . out . . . Woburn" (15). Woburn—but an object—tosses about on the sea. He is Echo's play toy, nature's thing, an unwilled object.

Such an elemental regression is essential to the meaning of the play. Unlike traditional quest patterns, where the hero represents in large the spectating audience so as to elevate human purpose and connect it to divine design, here the Beckettian non-hero is curiously nonrepresentational, and smaller. Woburn is bodied but not bodied-forth; born but not from his mother's womb; shaped not by experience but from the material of mud. Woburn's is a sea outing. It is wet, slimy, primal. Woburn seeks nothing: "no more trees . . . no more bank . . . he's changed . . . not enough . . . night too bright . . . soon the dunes . . . no more cover . . . he stops . . . not a soul . . . not—*Silence*" (Cas, 11). Truly, Woburn's struggle is a drag. And as he drags his huge bulk to the bank, his body actually begins to take on nature's shapes, until our literal sense of corporeality is forced to become more elemental, more metaphoric; that is, less humanly contoured: "what's in his head . . . hole . . . a shelter . . . a hollow . . . in the dunes . . . a cave . . . vague memory . . . in his head . . . of a cave" (11). It would seem that Woburn's elemental metamorphosis brings Echo into the very center of the play.

In her essay "Echo and Beauty," Patricia Berry writes about the psychic importance of empty space for creating deep meanings. She provides us with a reverie on caves, just as Bachelard had done on water, and by so doing enables us to see better the bond of nature with soul. She says, "Echo's aesthetic occurs in the empty spaces, the caverns. This emptiness—the emptiness in an event, the lack of manifestation—gives shape to Echo."[12] This aesthetic to which Berry is referring is mythic rather than philosophic and refers to Beckett rather than Joyce. Joyce, with his aesthetic of epiphany, borrows from Aquinas to suggest that events manifest meaning—suddenly, luminously, radiantly.[13] Manifestation gives shape to understanding and therefore to mind itself. But here a different aesthetic is suggested, where things do not, in new enlightening and lighter ways, manifest clearer and ever clearer meaning. With Beckett, rather, the "Echo aesthetic" condenses meaning. It condenses what we think we hear, making hearing heavier, less light. It muddies understanding. Beckett's aesthetic, where Echo lives and sounds, is what the psychological tradition might describe as "coagulation," wherein solid understanding is formed not from manifestation clarified but from presence thickened.[14]

In the seventies and eighties, Beckett more and more has focused his work on less and less. This move is consistent with an aesthetic founded on words that speak to the senses, re-sounding, re-iterating, echoing the syllables of sensory longing. In hearing again, we hear words of greatest, most fearful meaning broken into units of sound. We hear bits, traces. We hear air in consonants and consonance in air. What's it meant to mean? No more than Echo "means," no more than vowels "mean," no more than a horse's whinny.[15]

A play of elemental sounds, then, connects Beckett's characters with nature's air, earth, fire, or water. In *That Time* Beckett dramatizes "that time" (*illo tempore*) putting—as it were—his radio plays on stage, making what is heard a mythic moment for what is seen. An ancient character called "Listener" must listen as never before to the voices that come to him from three distinct parts of his past: from his childhood, his youth, and his manhood. Beckett stages the play so that only the old man's head is seen, all emphasis falling to the voices. Like Winnie in Beckett's *Happy Days*, his fleshly condition is secondary to the more real presences of memories and of the rounds the mind takes. As we look at the disembodied face of Listener, we face a mystery. In the manner of myth, this is *"Old white face, long flaring white hair as if seen from above outspread"* (TT, 28). It witholds more than it reveals.

Of the three voices that come to Listener—A and B and C—the third C voice is most appropriate for the myth of Narcissus and Echo. As the voice of an old narcissist who has severed himself from the springs of being, C echoes an old man's winters of discontent. C's "that time" refers to two moments of elemental coldness when, despite his pain of loneliness and despite his miserable condition of flesh, despite the hell of living on earth—something else suddenly and from nowhere changed him, utterly. The meeting of *this* defined, wintered condition with *that* sensory awakening forges the play's connection between reality and myth.

The first occasion when C sees he is never to be the same again occurs in a portrait gallery. Elements of cold, wet, and dirt cover the scene of an appropriate winterly winter, when *this* staid reality appears least likely to bloom into hope of *that* mythic one. Yet, astonishingly, a little miracle does occur: "till you hoisted your head and there before your eyes when they opened a vast oil black with age and dirt someone famous in his time some famous man or woman or even child . . . or princess of the blood black with age behind the glass where gradually as you peered trying to make it out gradually of all things a face appeared had you swivel on the slab to see who it was was there at your elbow" (TT, 30). Out of nothing, a face appears, like a thickened presence. C is "never the same after that" (31), transformed from being nothing into being an echo of something. His condition changes from not knowing who he was from Adam (32) to a condition of seeing, suddenly, visibly, a kinship with the "blood black with age"—not with blue bloods, but with more ancient blood lines who preceded white civilizations. C is in need of finding new, though old, blood lines, for his wintered condition in all-that-is-old has dried him up "till the words dried up and the head dried up and the legs dried up whosever they were or it gave up whoever it was" (33). The miracle is that, despite his severed condition, C finds in the glass of the portrait gallery an unexpected connection with humanity. This connection with that humanity is all-inclusive: male with female, old with young, black with royalty. Out of the dust, C "hoists" his head, setting sail from land and dust and ruin—from Adam—and leaves behind a hell of aridity: "eyes passing over you and through you like so much thin air" (36). It would seem that C's magic moment changes his very "atoms," transforming them at an elemental level, turning a single-celled atom, the ego self, into a coagulated other.

A second occasion for C's reawakened being—"never the same after that"—occurs in a public library. Edifice of communication, the library serves, as does the portrait gallery and the post office, as C's haven from hell. These havens become places C seeks to dry off from the rain ("always raining") and the winter ("always winter"). Like the other free "places you hadn't to pay to get in" (TT, 34), the library offers refuge "far from home" (34). But it is refuge of a "kind"—to borrow Beckett's freighted word—for even in the drying-off shelters, open to the public, one has the sense of Plato's cave: bodies chained inside the free place, people emprisoned inside space, no one looking at anyone. C's arrival inside the post office, bustling with a Christmas crowd, is archetypically hellish: "in off the street when no one was looking out of the cold and rain pushed open the door like anyone else and straight for the table neither right nor left with all the forms and the pens on their chains sat down first vacant seat and were taking a look round for a change before drowsing away" (35). Without punctuation it all flows together, thickening with rhyme, with Echo, with rhythm. Straights become rounds, chains "change" and "rain." The scene, too, thickens, by its cultural references (to Plato), by its play of opposites (straights with rounds), and by its sense of hell as a palpable void. Nothingness acquires spatial dimension, as vacant seats are taken and as no looks are exchanged, either left or right. Such vacuity begins to take on a corporeality of its own, echoing Echo.

Similarly, elemental opposites come together in C's venture to the library and suggest a tangible connection between invisibles and sensibles. Outside elements of aridity and damp are brought inside, for instance, when old derelicts, presumed to be male, sit silently at round tables, poring over pages, turning leaves of books. Rain pouring becomes old ones poring; dust turns to leaves: "sitting at the big round table with a bevy of old ones poring on the page and not a sound" (TT, 36–37). Metamorphosis can be attributed partly to Beckett's non-punctuated style, where meanings constantly change, and partly to his ambiguous use of nouns and prepositions. The old ones, for example, described as a "bevy" (a word connected with larks, quail, or women) do not actually pore "over" the page; they pore "on" the page, giving an impression not of eyes passing through the text or over the text but actually of hair raining down, poring onto the page, bringing outside elements in. The effect of rain (or larks) coming inside the library is Echo's effect of making that which is distant more real, of making that which is suffered more substantial, and even more musical.

In the library, C's endless rounds in the cold, the rain and the winter, year after year, become finally metaphorically real, not literally real. Something happens to C in the library. Although he is condemned to repeat his hellish rounds, something will make his repetitions more those of Echo—a doubling—and less those of ego—a cloning. C will continue to go round and round, but in the endless circularity, rounds will echo rounds—deepening rounds, making with each circle a thicker, more coagulated presence. The dust C sees in the library echoes dust he sees in the portrait gallery, dust to dust. The two scenes echo each other, the second making visible what the first merely sensed. The second scene of dust thus allows what is sudden and unreal to take a really sudden shape and to make the nature of things true on a metaphoric as well as a literal basis: "suddenly this dust whole place suddenly full of dust when you opened your eyes from floor to ceiling nothing only dust and not a sound only what was it it said come and gone was that it something like that come and gone come and gone . . . in no time gone in no time" (TT, 37).

Here, in a place full of dust, where no sound sounds nor any thing appears—just here, in the void—syllables echo and words repeat. No thing can clarify meaning. But dust, falling from air, fills space and takes on presence. The phrase "come and gone come and gone" embodies Echo's soul. For while she is not seen in certainty, yet she appears continually to the face of an old man. Her soul lives on in the very nature of things: in the stone of bones, in the turning of leaves, in the rounds of sound, forever.

4   Storytelling: The Stone of Cronus

In the myth of Cronus the sky god, when Cronus swallowed his children, he thought he was aborting a prophecy he could not stomach.[1] He thought, by using his head, he could prevent an overthrow by his children. One after the other Cronus gulped down Hestia, Demeter, Poseidon, Hera, and Hades. But the last born, Zeus, Cronus did not swallow. Tricked by his wife (also his sister) Rhea, Cronus swallowed not his child but a stone wrapped in swaddling clothes. The stone lay heavy in Cronus's stomach until his son grew to manhood and challenged the father's reign. This myth, classically—even chronically—Freudian, portrays a life and death rivalry between fathers and sons and depicts mothers in league with children.

Chapter 2 discussed the ways in which Cronus, a typical non-hero, features in the works of Beckett. Now we shall see how Cronus assumes deeper, more mythical proportions in Beckett's works. That the old man character of Beckett must tell stories, continuously, is an indication of his need not to live in chronology but to abandon time frames altogether. That the old man finds new life in fantasy is a tribute to the power of storytelling, which, like the stone of Cronus, lies heavy in the belly, waiting for rebirth.

So, at the end, when all else fails, the old man tells himself stories. "What I need now is stories," says Molloy (M, 13); "It's storytime, where was I?" intones Hamm (End, 48); Krapp listens to his opus, really the story of his shadow self; and in *Ohio Impromptu* Reader and Listener, each other's other, read to and listen from the open pages of the book of their life. This mythic book, or story, however, does not follow the sequence of lived time. Refusing forward movement, it contains little plot and less chronology. Rather, it interrupts a rational habit of mind, breaking tracked patterns of literal responses and logical assumptions. Accordingly, the old man is drawn into storytelling not so much to tell as to listen. But what do words say when there is nothing left to tell?

"Word-saying," indeed, comprises the heart of the dramatic situation in Beckett's drama. While storytelling, a familiar motif in Beckettian fiction, has been the subject of the critical writings of Judith Dearlove, Ted Estess, Bruce Kawin, and James Hansford (among others),[2] it is the drama that turns telling

41

into a listening act. As an archetype, the old man needs to put the facts of his life on stage so that he can play act with them. Other features of his being make him immediately recognizable as a type, particularly to a Beckett audience. He wears, typically, a long black coat or dressing gown, is bowed down with pain or fatigue, and has an extraordinary head. Either he has something wrong with his head (like Henry in *Embers*), or he has a heart in his head (like Hamm in *Endgame*), or the hair on his head has grown so long that, as Stan Gontarski suggests, "it seems to have grown for years beyond death."[3] Clearly, the head signifies not a thinking place but a place in which and through which story's words sound connections between present and past, life and death.

With this archetypal old man and his ritual story, Beckett achieves a wonderfully poetic, dramatic occasion, the basic building block of which is repetition: repetitive character, repetitive words, repetitive actions, repetitive scenes. Mircea Eliade, in his work on ritual, describes repetition in ways that relate strikingly with Beckett's drama of the storytelling old man. According to Eliade certain dance and song rites satisfy a basic human need to return to the roots of being. Repetitious movement and repeated syllables provide the means by which a celebrant can propel him or herself out of "this time," into that time, *in illo tempore*. As Eliade writes, "sacred time appears under the paradoxical aspect of circular time, reversible and recoverable, a sort of eternal mythical present time that is periodically reintegrated by means of rites."[4] In storytelling, the old man engages in just such a ritual recovery of being that, like the children in Cronus's stomach, requires constant regurgitation.

Three moments identify three turning points in storytelling, making the old man's obsessive need to speak an act of profound ritual importance. The first moment is that of regressing. The old man can't get certain words out of his head—"stone" and "ruin," for instance. The story he tells himself revolves around his words literally and figuratively and circles over them in maddening repetition. As an audience sees him pacing circles and hears him resaying his words, a dance of meanings combines language, action, and consciousness. Drama becomes a pulling in and a pulling down to where story's words are heard mindlessly, as in a koan. Truly, the words to which the self responds must empty of conceptual, or chronic, or mere meaning.

A second key moment in the rite of storytelling is encountering. Words, emptied of precise denotation by an act of eternal (infernal) repetition, evoke other presences. Figures, ghosts, images, memories—hoisted from the deep past—throw the old man back to where he can touch repressed pain. There, on the fields of imagination, language releases its "presential" power that hovers around the various connotations of spoken meaning. Among such presences, an old man's personal hell can transpose into a mythical Hades. But unlike the encounters of mythic heroes, Beckett's old man encounters are non-heroic, weakening rather than strengthening ego and all that the ego controls.

Patrick Magee as Hamm and Stephen Rae as Clov in the Royal Court Theater production of *Endgame,* London, 1976, directed by Donald McWhinnie. Reprinted by permission of John Haynes, photographer.

A third moment seldom reached in the early drama and only fleetingly reached in recent plays is the ritual moment of sensing. The old man's story, not just his to tell, transposes into Its to be listened to. Like a celebrant, the old man mediates two times—one sacred, the other profane—where a deeper dimension of being lives of itself. In Jungian terms this coming-to-life of soul, or anima, shares an affinity with animals and feels like a flame. Jung says, "It is something that lives of itself, that makes us live; it is a life behind consciousness."⁵ Jung's definition of soul as a deeper, lower livingness relates suggestively to Beckett's definition of language as "extraaudenary" (D, 293), evoking the unsaid by the said; or of memory as "involuntary," choosing its own time and place for the performance of its miracle (P, 19). When, thus, the old man experiences sensing, he is feeling the basic building blocks of story ("stone," "ruin") in new ways that allow him to touch—not just to think about—his childlike other self.

The old man's ritualistic need to tell stories has consistently occupied Beckett's dramatic writings. Three plays, covering three decades, demonstrate this consistency in ritual storytelling and reveal as well Beckett's use of the stage as a place of potential dramatic transformation. *Endgame*, *That Time*, and *Ohio Impromptu*—all chart an absolute necessity of the storytelling act for discovering the source of being. But the plays also illustrate Beckettian theater as uniquely integrative, wherein action on one stage transforms action to another stage, where audience acts with actor, becomes actor. Actors and audience alike must listen, listen, in a never-ending need to hear the words better. As same words are sounded repeatedly in new combinations, the actor's head empties and fills— like tides of the sea. What becomes dramatic is not physical action and grand gesture—out there—but internal leaps of imagination, within the active imaginations of both audience and actor.⁶

The original stage design for *Endgame*, by Jacques Noel, suggests this dramatic quality of enacted saying and its effect on consciousness. The stage, looked at from the audience, appears like a vast empty skull, with windows like eye sockets. As the characters wheel about the center, emptiness begins to acquire depth, and seeing acquires a listening dimension. With such emphasis on the head and the space emptied within it, the audience begins to function differently inside their own heads, either rejecting outright what they are experiencing in the theater or questioning their basic security systems.

Hamm, with a toque on his head like a hollow crown, resembles an old king defending his hollow ways. Similar to his predecessors Krapp, Henry, Pozzo, or Malone (from Beckett's fiction), Hamm—the archetypal, chronic, old man—carries the sense of an old ego into our modern world. Immobilized, his face covered with a large bloodstained handkerchief, his body draped with a sheet, he also reincarnates the figure in "Echo's Bones," who is about to set sail over the waters. These multiple associations converge to suggest that dying to the old order, the old ego, the old way—*that* dying—is the great project of rebirth.

Hamm's oldness points to pivotal change in two distinct ways. First, his decrepitude is such that his body fills with holes. He is a sieve, plagued by constant leakage. With holes for eyes (he is blind), he also has a hole in his heart and a gaping hole in his head, for which he requires a pain killer. "There's something dripping in my head. (*Pause.*) A heart, a heart in my head" he says (End, 18). Were it not for these holes, however, it would be impossible for an other order of reality to seep through; for these holes "crack" consciousness. Secondly, Hamm's language, a mix of literalism and fantasy, suggests his affinity with border situations. While he loves the comfort that an interpreted world can bring— the old questions, the old answers—he also has a fertile imagination. He thinks of the "beyond" as a place of green hills (39), and he remembers, with yearning, flowers in the field (42) and rising corn (44). When pushed to his limits Hamm reverts to story. Storytelling for this Cronus figure is a basic act of disgorging, of letting out that which makes one heavy.

The Unnamable referred to story as "incomprehensibly mine" (U, 413), where a storyteller can "be again." In accord with the original meaning of the word "reconciliation"—to return, to refind origins—storytelling accomplishes a fundamentally regressive act. The return takes one back to what lies on the other side of forgetfulness: first, or primal memories. It also returns one to an original place, where forgiveness can be found. In Greek myth the other side, or the underworld, has its own topography of fields and corn, known as the Elysian Fields. The Greek picture of this death place, abloom and fertile, suggests that to the Greek imagination when one dies one returns to a newer, greener life. When, therefore, Hamm goes back to story, he is regressing to something primal inside himself from which he is seeking forgiveness—his own swallowed child self.

The story setting, which emphasizes oldness, prepares an auditor to hear with the ears of a child. We are taken back to an early, old time when familiar ideas, stripped of old meanings, stand forth anew—as images. The setting, a deserted hole, both mirrors and deepens the stage setting, giving emptiness a depth in metaphoric image. The heart of the story, of course, concerns an early moment in Hamm's life as a child; but, against the setting in imaginary time, lived facts metamorphose. Concerning a feudal lord to whom paupers must make petition, the story enables Hamm to exercise power over the kingdom of his mind. It appears that one pauper, from a "hole" far away and uninhabited, now seeks aid for his child. Hamm, as lordly narrator, enjoys the role he gives himself in story and demonstrates distance from its situation of need by ridiculous verbal embellishments: "It was a glorious day, I remember"; "It was an extraordinarily bitter day, I remember"; "It was a howling wild day, I remember." Clearly, Hamm is only playacting, merely exercising word skills; true memory has not yet been engaged. Why such circumlocution? In moving around the moment of encountering, circling it with evasion and cleverness, Hamm forestalls memory's truth.

The pauper's petitioning question, which concerns the child, sharpens that point at which "telling" and "listening" converge. Drained by the efforts of bombast, Hamm in the midst of his own story readies to hear its question on more than one level. He indicates this shift in consciousness by employing images of the sea: "I don't know. (*Pause.*) I feel rather drained. (*Pause.*) The prolonged creative effort. (*Pause.*) If I could drag myself down to the sea! I'd make a pillow of sand for my head and the tide would come" (End, 61). Letting tides fill his head signals a moment in the telling when Hamm's role playing breaks down. Ceasing to play the role of tyrant, he can become a petitioner; ceasing to be the teller, he can become the told. Hamm readies himself for an encounter with the question: Would he consent to take in the child? (End, 53).

For Hamm to "take in the child" would be for him to regress in time to the feeling of the child when he, like the pauper's son in the story, had been abandoned by his father; when he, like his Biblical namesake, had inherited the curse of the father; when he, like Cronus's son, had been taken into his father's belly. Rather than literalizing the situation of his past, Hamm needs to fantasize its terror, returning the moment now to the fields of imaginative power then, until power and its opposite terror can change, shift, soften, give birth, create. If Hamm can bring himself to the brink of his story's question—Would he consent to take in the child—he could create living fantasy from mere chronicle. He could give birth to imagination.

Endgame, however, never quite gets inside its dramatic situation. Concluding his story, Hamm says, "Well, there we are, there I am, that's enough" (83). "Enough," apparently, is simple telling, when the "I" and the "me" never meet. At the end, Hamm covers his face with his handkerchief, recalling the suffering Christ. But psychic wounds have not sufficiently crucified imagination to allow holes of pain to seep like the sea into memory. Instead, holes are covered so as to staunch the flow of suffering: "Old stauncher!" Hamm says to his handkerchief at the end, "(*Pause.*) You . . . remain" (84).

That Time, more fragmented than *Endgame*, splits time zones off among three voices, speaking at the mercy of their memories. Katharine Worth made an important point about the play when she distinguished it not as "situation" but as "the sense of" situation—drama coming through sound and sensing.[7] Mythically, to the degree that it tells fewer chronicled events, drama intensifies. As storytelling becomes more impossible to perform, performance becomes more a listening-to, turning listening into action and action into listening. Beckett intends this shift in emphasis in *That Time*, as mentioned in chapter 3, by a stage setting that displays a face "floating in its white hair" in the middle of stage darkness, addressed by a voice from three different time periods and coming from three different stage locations. A, B, and C, the three speakers, together with the listening self called Listener, form four distinct aspects of selfhood: youth, midlife, maturity, and old age. The white-haired old man presents an image of the wise man figure of fairytale or myth, or perhaps an ancient sage of the East, Lao-tse or Confucius. But the anguish and apparent lack of comprehension on the old man's part suggest that wisdom can no longer be told or even narrated; it must be petitioned.

The voice of A tells of a time, "that time," when a child's loneliness seems like a dry hell among old ruins and sharp nettles. This moment echoes *Endgame*. Like the pauper's "hole," this place of the child's abandonment is empty, not at all a part of the living. Also like *Endgame*'s "situation at Kov" (End, 52), such an extreme aloneness creates the condition out of which fantasy is born. A learns make believe "talking to yourself who else out loud imaginary conversations . . . on a stone among the giant nettles making it up now one voice now another" (TT, 31). In addition, A speaks "imaginary conversations," dialoguing with other, earlier selves. But here, images of sharpness—the nettle and the stone— give loneliness texture, even place, suggesting that the child's extreme condition has its own dimension, its own boundary, of significance.

A's voice resounds with that of C, both voices relating a time, "that time," of desolation in maturity. C's hell is not so much a matter of being without humankind as it is being in the midst of others with whom one has no contact whatsoever: "eyes passing over you and through you like so much thin air" (TT, 36). The voice of C tells of an incessant quest to find touchstones between the self and culture. But civilized institutions, erected as foundations of external communication, provide no nourishment. Art galleries, churches, post offices, museums—C searches them all for validation that he is a real part of the mainstream. Only when he catches a glimpse of a face behind a glass in a picture gallery does he sense himself. This tiny moment reveals an enormous point. What holds the eye and fires the soul has nothing to do with the great works of famous people; what inspires the soul is simply one other's flicker onto one's own consciousness.

B, in the second stage of life, achieves a different return to an earlier place of being, where love and possibility teeter on the edge. The image clusters of B's story circle around the word "stone," mentioned four times and a fifth time in combination: "on the stone together in the sun on the stone at the edge of the little wood and as far as the eye could see the wheat turning yellow vowing every now and then you loved each other just a murmur not touching or anything of that nature you one end of the stone she the other long low stone like millstone" (TT, 29).

If, like Dante's quester, B can get beyond the hell of "that time," he must imagine differently. He must acquire an imagination of stone, feeling more sharply or keenly the child part of himself that has petrified his ability to respond. Jung once said, "The making of the stone is woman's work and child's play."[8] By connecting stone with the old man, Beckett implies a Cronus-like situation where all that is most fixed and hidden can still regenerate itself out of fixed conditions. This implication is borne out with the word "stone" that is anything but fixed in Beckett's text. It shifts according to which other word groups combine with it. Refusing single meaning, "stone" takes on doubleness, both as a place where being-alone is being-together-with and as a place where togetherness is lonesome. B's stone thus mediates the stone of A and C, uniting their separate fragments as two parts of a whole. Similarly, although in the fragment quoted above no touching or speaking occurs, the stone cements feeling. Even "millstone" continues this implicit doubleness; it carries the poetic vehicle both of what weights B down with mental burden, like millstone, and also of what grinds "wheat turning yellow," chaff to grain, like millstone. If B were to weigh his burdens differently, more imaginatively, he just might be able to see the grains of his own story's truth. Surely B's stone, like the philosopher's stone, like Cronus's stone, contains a poetry of oppositions!

Another of B's fragments in the ritual of storytelling connects "stone" with water—its natural opposite: "alone on the end of the stone with the wheat and blue or the towpath alone on the towpath with the ghosts of the mules the drowned rat or bird or whatever it was floating off into the sunset" (TT, 34–35).

B's story regresses further back in memory to an image of himself alone without his lover. On a literal level the image of death and desertion suggests closure of B's love, a world collapsed. On another level, however, dying produces multiplicity, fluidity, animation. Alone, B metaphorically accompanies ghosts. He shares his personal hell with bulky shapes that come before him in animal forms: mules, a rat, a bird. In listening, one hears more than a fragment of plot; one hears how "the blues" transcribe like a barge a mule pulls along the waters of a canal. B's story moves from the edge of a little wood to a towpath and from land to sea. And precisely because B's animal images are not empirical, real animals, they drag the soul.

B's final image cluster pushes Listener even farther back toward an encounter with self, where images animate deep consciousness. Darkness takes on density, enabling one to see into shades of meaning, and to hear words ring: "that time in the end when you tried and couldn't by the window in the dark and the owl flown to hoot at someone else or back with a shrew to its hollow tree and not another sound hour after hour hour after hour not a sound" (TT, 37).

This image deals directly with hollow space and its potential for fullness. Silence surrounds each word, not as mere silence, but as the sound of "no sound." Equally, darkness is not the absence of light, but the presence of another universe. For Beckett's poetics, night activates soul and requires thereby sharper seeing and shrewder hearing to sense its ways. In his "Peintres de l'empêchement" Beckett speaks to this point, describing true seeing as an acquired skill of night vision.[9] The final fragment of B's story suggests a need for Listener to awaken not to dawn but to night's dawn and to the dawning sense that night life creates.

Sensed thus, Listener could hear B's final image cluster as a hearing inside the hollow spaces of his own mind coming alive in animal fashion. Owl and shrew go together into the hollow space of a tree. An owl, symbol of wisdom and vision—keen with the eyes, asleep during the day—comes alive at night. It takes a shrew to its hollow tree, leaving us to imagine a deadly scene: owl feeding upon shrew. But together, owl and shrew form a composite; for a shrew, blind of eye and awake in day, senses with its nose—smelling at every corner. On one hand we can imagine a primal rite. On an other hand, we can imagine two sensory ways of being coming together, wisely, shrewdly, with clear sight and keen hearing. In such dying, we can imagine fierce livingness.

Feeling words as well as hearing them empowers the rites of story to reawaken sense. This story begins, after all, with a simple image—a man sits on a stone at the edge of a wood. But we need to see such a simple image in many ways: seeing its connection with the old man's literalism and obsessiveness, feeling a difficulty in its comprehension, and even listening to hear it. For it is the sounding of the "o" sound in "stone" re-sounding in the "no sound" of the final fragment that strikes the basic words of B's story: "no," "stone," "low," "towpath," "float," "ghost," "old," "flown." Out of such deep musical tones comes a flowing of sound that creates worlds of meaning. The stone as millstone implies stone as grindstone or brimstone, multiplying sense, until sound becomes a true touchstone of the self.

Finally, *Ohio Impromptu,* a recent minimalist drama, maximizes sound, drawing attention even farther into the listening rather than the telling act. As in *That Time* a character (called Listener) listens. But here Listener assumes a more active role, knocking with his left hand at key moments in Reader's narration. Knocking seems to accomplish two purposes: to interrupt the flow of the story's text (preventing Reader from overlooking phrases of importance, forcing Reader to reread) and to allow a pause between phrases. Listener, with his corrective knocks to consciousness, insists on spaces around words—proper empty spacing—so that the words may empty and fill with meaning. And the left hand does the knocking, because Listener's left side of intuition is in need of hearing words more keenly, less sequentially.[10] Listening requires a shrewd ear, for when "nothing is left to tell" (OI, 34) one must listen to what is "left."

Another room, another window, another sense of *in extremis* ties the dramatic situation of *Ohio Impromptu* to *That Time.* A past memory of the "dear one" and unspoken words haunt present time. Other ties to *Embers* describe an old man's torture as follows: "Nothing, all day nothing. (*Pause.*) All day all night nothing. (*Pause.*) Not a sound" (Emb, 121). In *Embers* Henry walks incessantly along the edge of the sea, alone, "just to be with me," and in being-with continues his unfinished story of Bolton and Holloway. As with the text-within-a-text of Reader and Listener, Henry's story within a story recounts a man who tells stories: "Stories, stories, years and years of stories, till the need came on me, for someone, to be with me, anyone, a stranger, to talk to, imagine he hears me" (Emb, 100). Storytelling, however, does not allay the pain of Henry's world; it only makes that pain keener: "Fire out, bitter cold, white world, great trouble, not a sound" (119). And, like Listener's knocks on the white deal table shared by Reader in *Ohio Impromptu*, what punctures the soundlessness of Henry's sterile world are sharp, hard sounds: Henry's walking "boots on shingle" (95), horses' hooves walking "on hard road" (104), and the music master's "blow of ruler on piano case" (107). It is as if hearing what is "left" demands sharp knocks to the ear, in the manner of the Zen master, striking blows between the shoulders during zazen.[11]

The night side of the old man's life, his terror, is described in *Ohio Impromptu* by Reader's text as follows: "In this extremity of his old terror of night laid hold on him again. After so long a lapse that as if never been. (*Pause. Looks closer.*) Yes, after so long a lapse that as if never been. Now with redoubled force the fearful symptoms described at length page forty paragraph four . . . White nights now again his portion" (OI, 31). "Terror" and "fear" (here in *Ohio Impromptu*) rather than "torture" and "anguish" (in *Embers*) suggest that an old man's pain has taken yet another turn. Reader seems at a loss to comprehend the words he reads, even though the text is his. Comprehension, the act of grasping ideas, utterly lacks function here. What, then, has caused the old man's nights to come alive with such vividness, in the absense of rational understanding?

Words, metaphors, images, sound—these build blocks of sensing, not common sense. When the senses reawaken, words fill and flow, becoming so much more than the thing signified. Reader's text pushes comprehension back from the "little" left to tell to the "nothing" left to tell, "where nothing ever shared" (29). The text forces Reader off the rock of literalism, nothing as "no thing," and washes his senses with new hearing. "Nothing ever" activates sharing, turning at the negative to a positive "ever shared"—forever sharing nothingness.

In the next "extraaudenary" passage, metaphor, sound, and sense converge around a description of the sea: "At the tip he would always pause to dwell on the receding stream. How in joyous eddies its two arms conflowed and flowed united on. Then turn and his slow steps retrace" (29). There is a setting sail to this place in this story—to the receding stream—where Listener can "dwell." He can, there, inside the text at the moment of story's regressing to the empty dwelling place, simply be or dwell. Water, too, has a dwelling or living quality with its joyous eddies and arms that seem to embrace and give comfort. No wonder the old man thinks deeply, dwelling on an image that, of itself, can turn pain to joy. So, too, does sound soften the mournful "o." Unlike *That Time*'s repetitive circling of "o," here a full range of vowel sounds plays within meaning, as in the title, *Ohio Impromptu*, where sound opens away from the long "o" in "Ohio" to other vowels in "Impromptu," seeming to play with and thereby create new sounds. Indeed, the words of this passage—descriptive of the sea as picture— also are descriptive of the sea as sound, moving in a flowing way back and forth in assonance between and among the syllables of words. Dwelling on this passage, one's mind dips to deeper depths, other worlds, different senses.

The moment of encountering brings the regressing moment back to where past fills with presence. In *Ohio Impromptu* the storied phrase "one night" signals an encounter when, much like "once upon a time," the then and the now come together, briefly and poetically: "One night as he sat trembling head in hands from head to foot a man appeared to him and said, I have been sent by—and here he named the dear name—to comfort you" (OI, 32). Traditionally, the Night Visitor symbolizes consciousness reawakening in dream. Beast reawakens Beauty to her two-sided nature, for instance, as Eros reawakens Psyche. Here, the night visitor revivifies multiple presences of figures from inside the old man's stories, told over time. This visitor, for instance, recalls Holloway in Henry's text, sent to relieve Bolton's pain (in *Embers*). He also suggests the "shade" in Reader's text—even Listener, himself—(in *Ohio Impromptu*). The night visitor becomes all of these, and more. Beckett's stories force an encountering with textual situations, where drama "plays" one text over and against another, contextually, continually.

Encounter as text-encounter inevitably draws attention to a dramatic potential of language itself. Beckett seems to take de Saussure's "langue et parole" distinction between "speech and speaking" even farther.[12] He seems to dramatize language as music, in the manner of what George Steiner wrote; namely, that language "passes into music" when it attains a "maximal intensity of its being."[13] The word "Impromptu" (in *Ohio Impromptu*) as a musical term and the encountering moment heard as a "second movement" bear out these musical notions (Gontarski, 133). This use of language relates with Phillip Wheelwright's *Metaphor and Reality*, wherein he makes reference to early man's experience of the world as a continual, hovering "presence."[14]

Such a presential use of language is dramatized in *Ohio Impromptu*. Across a plain white deal table on which is placed a book, two expressionless men *"as alike in appearance as possible"* (OI, 27) face each other without speaking. Beckett presents a dead image out of which we must create a text. What we have to work with is lastness, and ending: "So the sad tale a last time told they sat on as though turned to stone" (34). Vowels in this sentence "play" among consonants, softly—almost sweetly—while the two men give an image of each other "as stone." "No sound. So sat on as though turned to stone." Words repeat. The old man's stories repeat too, like stones of a past. But here in *Ohio Impromptu* stone and old man unite. Turning to stone, the old man becomes stone: unblinking, expressionless, nonhearing, nonseeing, mindless, childlike: "To sound of re-awakening. What thoughts . . . who knows what profounds of mind. Of mind-lessness. Whither no light can reach. No sound" (34). Circling around and around the same material—endlessly—words grind text, wear down the book in the center of the deal table (the volume is "worn"), softening meaning—until chaff becomes grain, stone mills stone, and mind reawakens to true mindless-ness. What do words say when there is nothing left to tell? *Ohio Impromptu* tran-scribes a koan to the drama of the stage where nothing is encountered. Beckett's old man never succeeds, as traditional mythical heroes do, with successful dragon battles and boon retrievals. We have moved off the stage of literalness. Rather, Beckett's ritual of storytelling accomplishes a much more difficult task. From *Endgame* through *That Time* to the recent minimalist work, the old man has strained his ears. His task is to be "holy"—not "to tell," but "to listen," until heads contain holes and petrified concepts turn to fancy.[15] His task is to feel the stone figuratively; that is, to let the heaviness inside lighten, to allow chronic melancholy to spill, even to spew forth, in stories that won't be stopped.

5   Measures of Despair: The Demeter Myth

To hear the old man tell stories is to hear myth come alive. We recognize in the old man's tales pieces of other Beckett stories, fragments of myth. Like the Greek word *mythos*, which refers to story or fable, the old man's stories concern imagination—not *logos*, or truth, not *khronos*, or time. As we saw in chapter 4, the stories old men tell give birth from the stomach and animate an old male soul.

In this chapter I will consider Beckett's women characters, who are mythic in quite another way.[1] Early reviews of *Not I* and *Footfalls*, the first of six plays which feature women, are refreshing in the manner the critics confess a wondering nonunderstanding of Beckett's women. Writing for the *New Yorker*, Edith Oliver said of *Not I*, "Something of great power and vividness—tatters of incidents and feelings, not a story but something—comes through from a dementia that is compounded of grief and confusion. I have no idea what the title means." Benedict Nightengale, reviewing the same play for the *New Statesman*, remarked, "The old woman's predicament strikes me as more moving than the old man's." And in commenting on *Footfalls*, Irving Wardle of the *Times* said: "I do not understand this play. . . . But simply in terms of stage imagery, and the sense of an indefinable, unassuageable grief, the impression is as potent as that Miss Whitelaw made in *Not I*."[2]

These critics draw our attention to the way women in the Beckett canon relate to myth. Women are in touch with a more mysterious, dark side of myth because they are more in touch with suffering. In ancient times, Mircea Eliade explains, a positive value was placed on suffering when initiates seeking an understanding of godly mysteries were made to undergo physical discomfort in order to achieve a higher state of being. Similarly, the alchemists considered suffering, and its transformation, the great work of wisdom. James Hillman, in summarizing cultural patterns of descent and resurrection in terms of psychic processes, insists on the significance of descent, inferiority, and despair for the renewal of the soul. And Matthew Fox discusses suffering as a gift of the *via negativa* because suffering allows for birth.[3] In traversing a negative way into suffering, then, women take us to another meaning of the word *mythos*, even farther from the *logos* of the old man's stories. Tom Moore, in writing of a second meaning of the

Greek word *mythos,* makes this point: "The other startling comment on myth we find in [the Greek lexicon compiled by] Liddell and Scott is this: myth is a story told to those who do not listen. . . . But there is, in fact, something suicidal, something self-destructive, about myth. Myth wants to be told and then destroyed. It wants to be heard but not listened to. The most dangerous, dark side of myth is that it is often a story heard and then not forgotten."[4] With these comments in mind, I will consider the primary function of grief in Beckett's women. And who expresses grief in myth better than Demeter, whose relation to earth is dark and deep.

Demeter, Greek goddess of grain and measure (Da-meter), is fascinating both because of her bounty and her grief. While on the one hand she represents all that the goddess as earth mother can be, bringing grain to humanity, she is also the epitome of a *mater dolorosa,* whose despair at the loss of her daughter, Persephone (Proserpine in Roman myth), knows no bounds. In this one figure of Demeter opposites unite. Earth and underworld, daughter and mother, giving and losing, body and soul—all come together, each a "grain" of truth. When men and women celebrated Demeter's rites in the Eleusinian mysteries, they gave recognition to the role despair plays in transforming human affairs.

It should come as no surprise, then, that allusions to Demeter are woven into the very fabric of Beckett's texts. Perhaps more than any other twentieth-century writer, Beckett taps the depths. And Demeter's paired relation with her daughter, Persephone, taps an archetypal structure of the psyche that Beckett shows in various configurations (mother-daughter, father-son, old man-young boy). Her story, primarily one of loss, is Beckett's basic story. Her journey to find the lost one, paradigmatic of the Beckettian search, becomes at the same time a journey to find a lost part of the self. It is an anxious quest, a way of sorrows, a *via dolorosa,* forcing the quester to live as never before—on the edge. A usual way of being is invaded, suddenly, without cause or provocation, bringing new relations and establishing new terms of need. We witness the travail of *Lost Ones,* living *All Strange Away,* in a *Come and Go* pattern that makes them *Ghost Trio*(s)—to themselves, to us.[5] Beckett's titles capture a haunting female *mythos* that can neither be forgotten nor understood.

Early in his writing Beckett refers to the myth of Demeter in the twelfth poem from his 1937–39 collection of poems.[6] Shadows, voices, and the plains of Enna recall first obliquely then directly the rape of Demeter's daughter:

> jusque dans le cavern ciel et sol
> et une à une les vieilles voix
> d'outre-tombe
> et lentement la même lumière

qui sur les plaines d'Enna en long viols
macérait naguère les capillaires
et les mêmes lois
que naguère
et lentement au loin qui éteint
Proserpine et Atropos
adorable de vide douteux
encore la bouche d'ombre.[7]

Basic to this (untitled) poem, as to the myth of Demeter, is a dynamic tension between sun (sol) and shadow (ombre), maidenhair (capillaires) and Proserpine, cavern and mouth (bouche)—a tension that focuses on the central image of "raped maidenhair" ("en longs viols macérait naguère les capillaires"). Subject-object ambiguities so pervade the poem that language obscures rather than clarifies meaning. If "longs viols," or long rapes, refers to a relation of light to maidenhair fern; the phrase functions merely metaphorically to suggest sunlight "raping" the meadows of Enna (les plaines d'Enna) with a fierce intensity of light. But if the image refers to specifics of the Demeter myth, it functions both literally (to suggest an invasion of maidenhair) and metaphorically (to suggest a violent thrusting-together of life and death patterns).

Obscurities of meaning are further built into the fabric of this poem with unpunctuated endlines, repeated "ands," and with the final "encore." Sky and sun form, at first, a cavern, seeming to make the outer world a smaller part of a larger "hole." At the end of the poem the cavern forms a new shape, a mouth of shadow ("la bouche d'ombre"), as if the hole of the cavern's darkness were now swallowing itself. Beckett suggests that the big world of sky's cavern will again become the little world of shadow's mouth—perhaps that sky fathers will yield to earth mothers; that is, be reborn (metaphorically) from the speakings of women ("les vielles voix," "la bouche d'ombre"). Or that the macrocosm ("d'outre-tombe," "le cavern ciel et sol") will be eaten up by the microcosm ("la bouche d'ombre")—the big world entombed by the small world. Instead of rape of the female (the structuring metaphor of the poem), there is the suggestion of engulfment by the female, alongside the suggestion of metaphorical rebirth.

Light and dark symbolism, consequently, exchanges its traditional association—light with pure, or unadulterated good, dark with pure or unadulterated evil—and complicates meaning. Light ("la même lumière") becomes a natural violator, cancelling out the shadow world. It is in the shadow world where the old voices ("les vieilles voix") live; they will be slowly and inexorably extinguished ("et lentement au loin qui éteint") like rays of light by the darkness inside the skull or cavern of the sky ("le cavern ciel"). Such extinguishing of the ancient voices in the context of the poem functions metaphorically ("les mêmes lois") like rape in that too much light or clarity ruins that which cannot be explicated clearly.

This early poem of Beckett's sets the stage for a feminine *mythos* that celebrates the various shades of darkness and intensifies the power of metaphor. Beckett presents forces that "macerate" an otherwise "exquisite feminine greyness"[8] such as that held by Proserpine and Atropos. Yet, paradoxically, these mythic women are capable of their own macerating, or raping, functions in their searches to inhabit strange territory. Atropos (the thread cutter) and Proserpine (the raped one) are perhaps two of the most terrifying female mythic figures who, because they sever or are severed from connection with the earth, bind themselves more deeply into darkness.

Thirty years after he wrote his French poem focusing on the daughter of Demeter, Beckett began to stage plays featuring women. All of them connect with the basic female myth of Demeter. Winnie, in *Happy Days*—the first play to feature a woman—shows the effect of being disconnected from the female source when exposed to too much light. Discovered in blazing sunlight, surrounded by an *"expanse of scorched grass"* (HD, 7), Winnie is cut off from the wellspring. In a Los Angeles production of the play (1986) directed by Allen Mandell, Winnie seems buried not in the earth but in the moon.[9] The effect illustrates Winnie's disassociation from all female symbols, even from the moon, and suggests that Winnie's story will birth no newness. Nevertheless, when Winnie tells her story of the mouse and the steep stairs, with such recognizable Demeter motifs as the "scream" and "underthings," we begin to get a sense of Demeter at work in her speaking—albeit at a parodic level. For only then do we see that Winnie's deep forgetting propels her down the literal stairs of Mildred's story ("descended all alone the steep wooden stairs, backwards on all fours, though she had been forbidden to do so" [HD, 55]) into a metaphorical scene of seduction, forcing relations—however furtive—with underworld consciousness.[10]

Beckett's plays of the seventies and eighties have become more and more associated with female characters (*Not I, Footfalls, Come and Go, Rockaby*). It appears that as Beckett's women move deeper into the shadows they follow a dynamic of his early poem (quoted above) where suffering is mouthed, spoken, felt, and moves us into a world where image takes control. Imagination moves even the body, so that in body—in lips, eyes, feet—we come to feel anguish, imagining it palpably. To fully understand this female dynamic, however, with its deeply mythic undertone, requires a brief look backwards.

"The Homeric Hymn to Demeter" recounts Hades' abduction of Persephone and Demeter's frantic searching. Clearly, it is an early expression of the psychic bonding mother and daughter share.[11] The setting, the plain of Nysa, is

A statue of Demeter seated, from the Sanctuary of Demeter and Kore at Cnidos, c. 340–339 B.C. Photograph reproduced by courtesy of the Trustees of the British Museum.

a grassy meadow where Persephone plays with twenty-four water nymphs far from the ear of her mother (ll., 5–6; 416–24). The daughter reaches to pluck a narcissus flower when suddenly the earth opens, and she is borne down into the underworld by Hades (ll., 15–20; 426–30). Her screams are heard by no mortal (ll., 24; 430); but her mother hears them as echoes which ring out from the heights of the mountains to the depths of the sea (ll., 36–37). Seized by anguish, Demeter searches for Persephone nine days and nine nights, carrying two torches (ll., 48–9). Anyone who sees her sees grief personified, for the long dark cloak that hangs from her shoulders is sadness itself. On the tenth morning of her search Demeter learns that Persephone has been abducted into the underworld to become its queen. Angry, Demeter sits near the Maiden Well in the town of Eleusis (ll., 97–98). She gains employment in the town, tending the child Demophöon at night. But by day she sits in a chair grieving, without speaking, smiling, eating, drinking, or washing.

The first part of the tale, filled with images of dryness and hardness, shows that life's flow is buried with the daughter in the underworld. Demeter's grief is also buried within her, needing only to flow in tears to release its neurotic hold on her consciousness. When the mortals for whom she works fail to recognize her as the goddess she is, she hardens her anger even further by causing a drought and making infertile all of the earth's surfaces (ll., 309). Like the well near which she sits, Demeter is a stone shell. She must learn to tap the springs of the well water as Cronus touched the stone. The end of the tale speaks didactically of needing to see beneath surfaces, to feel life's flow: "Happy is he among men upon earth," the poet says, "who has seen these mysteries" (ll., 480). Without insight into one's anger, in other words, life on earth is hell. To "know happiness," in Beckett's words, is to have "grace to breathe that void."[12]

In image as well as in theme the myth of Demeter touches the core of Beckett's work. His plays, particularly *Not I*, *Footfalls*, and *Rockaby*, bear an astonishing similarity to the motifs of Demeter. All follow a rhythm of Demeter's sorrowful search as a cycle of finding and losing. All connect the seasons of winter and spring with states of being. All show that unconscious life is more powerfully intense than conscious life. And, in all, mythic moments of regressing, encountering, and sensing, which have formed a questing pattern of Beckett's male characters, take on new urgency as women search literally for the metaphors that ground them.

In *Not I*, for example, a female character called Mouth takes us back to the "mouth" or source of suffering. The play, which lasts only fifteen to seventeen minutes, throws us into a Demeter situation of barren grief. We hear of a hellish life lived without the springs of emotion, "always winter some strange reason" (N, 22). But, just when life seems most lost, at rock bottom, the wellspring gushes forth from Mouth's lips. It is, in accord with Beckett's design, a play with "blubbering lips" that works "on the nerves, not the intellect."[13] Life that had contained no feeling on one level is suddenly assaulted by another life buried in another level. Buzzings and flickerings in the head spew forth as if from a burst dam. Broken fragments of sentences, interruptions, corrections, and frenzy thrust themselves upon Mouth unannounced. Something, a "dull roar in the skull" (N, 16) begging to be "let in," simply refuses to dry up.

The Persephone-Demeter motifs in *Not I* are too numerous to mention individually, since they occur on every page of the play's text. Nevertheless, the following examples give an idea of the pattern, which ushers an audience, as well as the silent character called Auditor, into an "unfathomable mind" (M, 106). Persephone motifs include references to *grassy meadow*, found in Beckett's use of "field," and "Croker's Acres" (N, 15, 20); references to the *suddenness* of the rape event, found in Beckett's phrase "suddenly she felt" (18) and "sudden flash" (16, 19, 21, 22); and references to the *scream*, as in Beckett's words "roaring" and "screaming" (16, 17, 21, 23). Demeter motifs include references to *constant walking*, as in Beckett's phrase "ferreting around" (21), and words like "on" and "back" (22, 23); references to *anguish*, as in Beckett's mention of tears (21) and madness (22); references to *sitting*, *staring*, as found in Beckett's phrase "long hours of darkness" (22) and his description of Mouth's insentience (15), motionlessness (18), and speechlessness (21). A further dynamic both of the myth and of Beckett's play is the need of opposites to combine, as in Beckett's *winter-spring* images (17, 22, 23). Also, the specific Demeter mythologem of *dry streams* is transposed in Beckett as a "flaw in her make-up" that so disconnects the "machine" that Mouth becomes "powerless to respond," "numbed," until "all that moisture" stills the brain (17); and again, as her attempt to "tell . . . then rush out stop the first she saw . . . nearest lavatory . . . start pouring it out . . . steady stream . . . mad stuff . . . half the vowels wrong . . . no one could follow" (22).

In keeping with the Demeter *mythos*, what happens to Mouth in *Not I* reflects what happens to an audience: we are made to hear calls for help as a summons to enter deeper levels of being. *Not I* puts an audience on edge, indeed; but what it does to an actress is even more extreme.[14]

Neither *Footfalls* (1976) nor *Rockaby* (1981) challenges an audience's nerves as does the 1972 play *Not I*; nevertheless, both bring out further dimensions of the Demeter myth. In both, the voice of a woman is what compels interest. In both, bodies seem ghostly. May, for instance, in *Footfalls*, is described as having "dishelleved grey hair, worn grey wrap hiding feet, trailing" (F, 42); while *Rockaby*'s Woman is described as "prematurely old. Unkempt hair. Huge eyes in white expressionless face" (R, 21). And, in both, there is a remarkable similarity to Beckett's plays of the same years that involve male characters who interact with male voices (*That Time*, 1976, and *Ohio Impromptu*, 1981). But what is of interest in these later plays of Beckett is that the main on-stage characters are always skewed: either "slightly off centre" (R, 9) or "a little off centre audience right" (F, 42). Not centered literally, the characters are removed also spiritually and psychically from the center of their being.

It is precisely this sense of distance from the center that connects Beckett's women to the myth of Demeter. Split off from their inner cores, their souls, these Beckettian characters have become mere shells or ghosts. A voice, to which they must listen, torments them with memories of failed connections and painful desires. By forcing its claim on body, the voice speaks of "it all," the pain of "it all," "revolving" in the mind (F, 44, 46, 48). As in the Demeter myth these Beckettian women begin to feel pain differently, in a way that nourishes or bodies forth soul.

Clearly, any Aristotelian notion of character, complete in body, capable with speech, conquering time with action, is overturned here. What is most characteristic of Beckett's women characters is not their presence but their absence. They have moved to another zone. The recent women characters, particularly, seem less whole in body than even Watt or Winnie. May, in Footfalls, not only has "poor lips" (F, 43) a "poor head" (46), and a "poor mind" (48), she also has a poor appetite, able to eat only a few "half-hearted mouthfuls" (47). The Woman in Rockaby, robbed even of named identity, neither talks nor acts. Her only utterance, the word "more," sounds (as Billie Whitelaw pronounced it) like "maw," to suggest a mouthing need for nourishment. These people appear famished because they are: they are starved for soul. Feeling their psychic voids as a deep inner hunger, they are reduced to minimal action, walking and rocking.

Such motions of back and forth, up and down—the movements of Demeter's psyche—are also the patterned rituals of Footfalls and Rockaby. According to Mircea Eliade, ceaseless repetitive acts, like walking and rocking, can have the effect of making sacred that which is profane. Inside "sacred space" time can be reversed. A person performing ritual action can transform time backwards, or downwards, to where the inhabitants of an other world (ghosts, voices, souls long dead) reside.[15] In identifying three steps whereby actions become ritual processes of transformation, Eliade relates strikingly with three moments Beckett's characters experience. These correspondences suggest that Beckett's work is new in old ways.

The first ritual step Eliade describes is the creation of a "threshold," which separates two time modalities, the sacred from the profane. Like regressing, this step requires that characters "fall" from fleshly conditions to allow for a renewal of the soul. Second, Eliade describes a "nocturnal regime," similar to encountering, wherein characters come face to face with darkness, seeing its contents as totally other. Third, Eliade describes a basic "con-fusion" when the two modalities meet, which is similar to the moment of sensing or reawakening. These three ritual conditions have special, urgent significance for Beckett's old women who, like Demeter and Persephone, exist in one world but live in an other.

In both *Footfalls* and *Rockaby*, a threshold between two modes of reality is situated in the speaker's particular time span in profane life on earth. May, in the first play is in her forties (F, 44)—although her appearance would suggest she is older or without age. She is, in other words, at the time of midlife crisis when body is midway through its journey in life. The soul, normally entombed during periods of light and wakefulness, begins to stir. Murray Stein explains this phenomenon in terms of liminal or threshold awareness: "What seems to come to fuller consciousness during midlife liminality is . . . an awareness of psyche . . . the soul that is otherwise dormant and invisible in the bright light of waking consciousness. Consciousness of soul, or soul-consciousness, seems to be the chief product of midlife liminality."[16] Stein goes on to describe this midlife liminality as ghostly: "The journeyers, or floaters, feel ghostlike, even to themselves . . . 'Ghost' is equivalent to 'soul,' and in liminality the soul is awakened and released . . . [and] a person . . . ventures into psychological regions that are otherwise unknown, inaccessible, or forbidden" (136). May, in her forties, is thus really in the springtime of psychic life, when body becomes less important than soul.

Rockaby's Woman, at an opposite season of time from May, is yet like May in her incessant to and fro movings. Sitting in her chair (French word for flesh), Woman seeks to rock herself out of a fleshly condition as she listens to Voice's words. "Fuck life," Voice says (R, 20). Life, a profanity, lacks the sacred dimension. As a mantra at the threshold, Woman utters her single word "more," imploring "more" to usher from the darkness.

Threshold existence in these two plays is also signalled by a difficulty both women have in communicating, as if they speak a language understood only by the dead. Both plays feature a woman whose Voice (another character), like the buried ghost of self, is but dimly understood. In *Footfalls*, for instance, Voice (Mother) has difficulty understanding May (the daughter). Beckett structures the play around echo technique to enhance an essential mystery of two levels that communicate by con-fusing sense. Mother and the daughter echo each other; one seen, the other heard. Heard in the play as Voice, Mother tells a story about her daughter, seen in the play as a Demeter image of despair. Trying to tell May's story, however, Voice (Mother) must constantly interrupt herself with the phrase, "What do you mean? What can you possibly mean?" The audience, too, enters this mysterious scene, wondering what can it possibly mean, this going around in circles? What we see (a half-human figure) and what we hear (a "semblance" of story) troubles our minds. Two levels, two consciousnesses, two stages of drama interact: one out there, the other in here, one up in the head, the other down in the feet. Clearly, echo structure is basic to the play's deep meaning, as Beckett's stage directions indicate: *"Chime a little fainter. Pause for echoes. Fade up to a little less on strip. Rest in darkness"* (F, 45). The task for the audience—to fill "the rest" in the darkness of our own heads—forces us to the brink of an absolute threshold of self.

Typical of Beckett's characters, May is haunted by loss. Her obsessive pacing up and down nevertheless seems a kind of therapy-by-instinct, for unable to mean anything to others—even to her own mother—she attempts to create meaning with her feet and with her words. Hers is literally a night story: it is about the nocturnal regime. Her pacing, a Demeter dance of despair, reflects a need to move "about" the night, until its claim can be registered in her body, felt deeply in her mind. The story is this: an old Mrs. Winter one autumn evening sits down to supper for which she has little appetite and asks her daughter her opinion on the Evensong service. Was it not strange? Her daughter disagrees:

> Mrs. W: You yourself observed nothing . . . strange? Amy: No, Mother, I myself did not, to put it mildly. Mrs. W: What do you mean, Amy, to put it mildly? . . . Amy: I mean, Mother, that to say I observed nothing . . . strange is indeed to put it mildly. For I observed nothing of any kind, strange or otherwise. I saw nothing, heard nothing, of any kind. I was not there. (F, 48)

This chilling tale of nonunderstanding and dead-end communication contains in the middle the daughter's question: "Just what exactly, Mother, did you perhaps fancy it was?" (47, 48). The word "exactly" juxtaposed with the word "fancy" and then "perhaps" is wonderfully fecund. It suggests, at the center of this barebones world, at the heart of autumn's night, that "fancy," only a "perhaps," nevertheless energizes psychic departure. This becomes apparent as May slips out "at nightfall and into the little church" (46), where she takes on the image of Demeter: "The semblance. (*Pause. Resumes pacing. Steps a little slower still. After two lengths halts facing front at R.*) The semblance. Faint, though by no means invisible, in a certain light. (*Pause.*) Given the right light. (*Pause.*) Grey rather than white, a pale shade of grey. (*Pause.*) Tattered. (*Pause.*) A tangle of tatters. (*Pause.*) A faint tangle of pale grey tatters. (*Pause.*) Watch it pass— (*pause*)—watch her pass before the candelabrum how its flames, their light . . . like moon through passing . . . rack" (47). Such happenings of "fancy" transport events and turn them into images, *logos* into *mythos*. Calling her story a "semblance," May knows it tells of an experience only half understood, ill seen ill said, about things not-there (the Holy Ghost at Evensong, the daughter Amy's absent presence). Even so, in telling it May is nourished, for images feed her soul. Like the *mythos* that racks her, like Plato's racked soul, May must "feed upon the food of semblance."[17]

A similar situation is seen with Woman in *Rockaby*, who also on the edge of all possible relationship, also needs "fancy" to feed her soul. Here the difficulty is not within the relationship of mother and daughter, but within the human species itself. Woman, simply, can find no other face, no other body, no other pair of eyes, to validate her existence. Her search is pathetically modest.

Billie Whitelaw as May in the Royal Court Theater production of *Footfalls*, London, 1976, directed by Samuel Beckett. Reprinted by permission of John Haynes, photographer.

All she seeks is "one blind up," one other window open, where one "a little like" herself can mirror back to her, herself—some tiny validation that she exists. At the window threshold, however, there is no other. It now becomes clear that if she is to find an other, she must look beyond subjects to objects. Perhaps there, in objects, she will find the "more" she so desperately seeks.

The two women in *Footfalls* and *Rockaby* share a second ritual act, which is the making of space for soul. Because they are out of the center the women must make sacred their off-center place, circumscribing it until "more" can come forth. In *Footfalls*, space is created by the act of walking. May must not only feel her feet, she must also hear them, however faint they fall. A need to hear and touch is what Katherine Burkman calls "negative epiphany," or showing what cannot be spoken "exactly."[18] Feet, thus, literally define: they limit, and by so doing, create space.

We see on stage a character visibly saddened at the same time we hear a rhythmic tread of feet. Only a strip of stage is lighted, so that as we strain to see, understanding comes to us through hearing basic sounds. A measured touching of feet to the ground transforms a sight of anguish into a sound of beauty. What we see is a slow dance, what we hear is a cadenced pace, drawing our listening eyes into its rhythm, the beauty of which is strangely at odds with the vision of despair.

May creates space beyond the center by pacing nine steps and making left-turn circles. A woman with dishevelled grey hair, wrapped in long grey tatters, she walks up and down. By so doing she reenacts the mystery rite of Eleusinian initiates, who, themselves, reenacted the pattern of Demeter's grieving. Theirs was the way of the wrong direction, a *via negativa*, a counter-clockwise move into the sinister realm of left-footedness.[19] Initiates prepared themselves for their search to understand grief patterns by imitating the precise actions of Demeter's search. Like her, they fasted, dressed in long robes, sat on stones. At the climax of the mysteries a day-long procession wound its way dancing and singing from Athens through the pass of Daphni onto the Eleusinian Plain, circling around, until at evening they arrived at the temple of Demeter. There a grief dance was performed by moving to the left. In a recent study of these rites, the circle to the left is described as follows: "First, we come to the Virgin's well, called the Kallichoron, 'well of the beautiful dances.' The circular well, protected by the outer wall of the sanctuary, is surrounded by stone pavement. Here circle dances are performed. Surely, the form of the dance is a circular movement to the left, counter to Demeter's upperworldly sense."[20]

Needing to feel grief as a left side of being, controlled by right brain activity, Eleusinian initiates needed to counter ego or "upperworldly sense." The point is emphasized by Patricia Berry: "Demeter consciousness tends to live life in a natural, clockwise direction; whereas to connect to her daughter she must begin to live in a contra-naturam, counter-clockwise manner as well. Kerényi (*Essays on a Science of Mythology*, p. 134) remarks how the rituals 'if danced in honor of Persephone would have to go as it were in the *wrong direction*, that is, to the left, the direction of death.' "[21]

Indeed, May draws her circle of nine steps in a sequence Beckett makes specific:[22] *Strip: downstage, parallel with front, length nine steps, width one meter, a little off centre audience right. Pacing: starting with the right foot (r) from right (R) to left (L), with left foot (l) from L to R. Turn: rightabout at L, leftabout at R. Steps: clearly audible rhythmic tread* (F, 42). Beckett's carefully choreographed stage directions serve an ancient mystery function of directing audience attention to where it may not wish to go; namely, in the direction of death. May's deliberate pacing to the left for nine steps acts as a kind of invocation, leading us also back and down (*sē-ducit*) into a nocturnal regime of soul. Needing to hear—not simply to move—her feet, May, too, must fully sense the space she is creating. She must get (back) in touch with underworld life. When she paces and circles on a narrow strip of stage she draws a circle of herself: She is May, daughter-mother in one; May, whose anagram Amy forms another character in the play world that confronts us. But she is also May, the real mother of Beckett; May, the springtime that disappears and comes again; May, the lost youth of ourselves that is our wellspring and our despair.

A similar encountering of the night space of the soul is seen in *Rockaby*, when Voice—rather than feet—paces Woman through nine sequences. Like May's feet, Woman's voice turns back on itself at a precise point, which prohibits story from getting ahead of itself and forces images to do rightabouts and leftabouts. The phrase that signals Voice's turn, repeated nine times in the text, is "all eyes/all sides," each turning seeming to locate the eyes progressively lower, until seeing (and hearing) become sensed no longer in the head but in some lower region of bodily awareness, in the feet, perhaps. The first three times, the voice turns on the phrase "going to and fro/all eyes/all sides" (R, 9, 10); the fourth time the pattern breaks to "going to and fro/all eyes like herself/all sides" (10); while the ninth and final turn of phrase is "she so long all eyes/famished eyes/all sides" (19). Each turning of the text, no matter which variation, contains the phrase "high and low" to suggest a synchronistic movement both of eyes searching high and low and of chair rocking high and low. The effect is curious, for although Woman's eyes remain unblinking, Voice tells us they are constantly active; and although the chair is inanimate, it comforts with encircling arms. These regressive Beckettian moves of sensory awareness downwards from mind into body and from subject into object thickens the dimensions of soul, giving soul new body, racking body with soul.

Voice's final utterance creates further depth dimension by the word "down"—repeated twenty-one times in four different segments, as if calling Demeter down to join Persephone. The harshness Woman sees and feels—"going down/right down" to where life is "fucked"—is made more complicated by encircling repetitions. Yet with each "down" the meaning changes slightly, until finally a different kind of meaning is felt: one less mean, more kind:

> So in the end
> close of a long day
> went down
> in the end went down
> down the steep stair
> let down the blind and down
> right down (R, 17) . . .
> close of a long day
> went down (19)
> down the steep stair
> let down the blind and down
> right down
> into the old rocker
> and rocked
> rocked
> saying to herself
> no
> done with that
> the rocker
> those arms at last
> saying to the rocker
> rock her off
> stop her eyes
> fuck life (20)

Words rocked from their literalness in noun permanence become fluid, as here. "Down" becomes not just a deep place but a soft place, composed of the small, light stuffings of memory and regret. Chair becomes fleshlike, capable of lulling or fucking.

As a third moment of ritual expression in Beckett's recent plays, a valuing of the thing turns orthodox patterns and hierarchies upside down. Objects rather than subjects contain the "more"; objects take the place of language, since they are ringed with embedded layers of meaning that call forth the centuries and bring back the ghosts. What communicates is not language heard serially, in sentences; exactly, in definitions; or fictionally, in stories. Rather, what communicates, in this third confounding moment, is a language of thingness that presents itself dumbly to our senses.

This turning to objects as a "kind" of meaning—often unkind and mean—is, of course, evident in Beckett's work throughout. From Lucky's bones and the tree in *Godot*; from Winnie's bag; from Krapp's tape; from Molloy's stones: objects become touchstones of true existential meaning for starved Beckettian souls. In *Company*, the work many consider Beckett's autobiography (discussed in the next chapter), selfhood is defined by objects which assume an iconic power of what Suzanne Langer calls "semblance."[23] By simply gazing at a blade of grass or observing the shape of a buttonhook, the narrator of *Company* glimpses an other dimension, apart from familiar time and place, and in that brief glimpsing apprehends a world of moreness, of the soul. Objects contain what subjects do not: multiple, imprecise meanings and metaphors without bound.

Rockaby's Woman is case in point. The subjects in her world have all deserted her. Left by herself in her rocking chair *"slightly off centre audience left"* (R, 9), she is like Winnie twenty years later, whose search down the steep stairs seduces her into the depths of myth, into the realm of Persephone, into her own imaginal space. Down she must go if she is to recover her soul which lies buried in her shell; for her life lies in death, where the seeds of rebirth are stored. Demeter's myth shows us, as does Beckett, that what must die is the old ego, with its dry, literal way of seeing.

In *Rockaby*, Woman is placed in a Demeter situation of dry search. Day after day at her window Woman looks for a face in the pane—as does the generic character A in *That Time*, also character B, also character C: each a one searching for an other. But the other does not appear on a literal level. Beckett's response is that because company cannot be found with subjects, objects at least make the solitary condition clear. This truth prepares a character to become a different kind of being—an artist, rather than a tourist, a quester in search of soul.

Accordingly, Woman's "sole" companions are windows and chairs. The windows, blinded, do not provide eyes to the soul but rather mirror back a stark and barren truth: "a blind up/like hers/a little like/one blind up no more" (R, 15–16). Facing other windows, Woman faces only blind sightedness, like her own; other panes, like her own pains: "behind the pane/another living soul" (16). Beckett suggests that only in pain can soul be seen, as through a glass, clearly. Yet, for Woman, it is time she stopped searching, for the "only" windows of *Rockaby*, like the "perhaps" fancy of *Footfalls*, yield only further confusion.

And yet, con-fusion is a beginning point in depth. There can be no "stopping." Woman pronounces the need to stop; but, to hear Billie Whitelaw pronounce Woman's phrase "time she stopped," a one-syllable word "stopped" extends on the lips for three syllables and a miracle is performed. The point is crucial, at the crux of Beckett's mythic intention: for precisely when it is "time to stop" another time sequence takes over, with a *mythos* not a *logos*, and a world of deeper time dimension floods the gates.[24]

So is it any wonder, really, that Woman's chair should offer Woman something "more"? For it is tangible, unlike the fleeting others. Inside her rocking chair, dressed in "best black" (R, 17), Woman derives comfort from its encircling arms. As in the French "pain" for bread, the object world becomes the very staff of life. Comfort denied by subjects is given freely by objects, as Beckett's stage directions indicate: *"Chair: Pale wood highly polished to gleam when rocking. Footrest. Vertical back. Rounded inward curving arms to suggest embrace"* (22).

But objective reality in Beckett is not the opposite of subjective reality, just of a different kind. In *Footfalls* Beckett uses a strange noun. May paces up and down, up and down, he writes, like "moon through passing . . . rack" (F, 47). The word "rack" signifies, first, a framework or stand for the display of articles; second, a toothed bar that meshes with another toothed bar, such as a pinion or gearwheel; third, a framelike instrument of torture. Other meanings of "rack" relate familiar Beckettian themes, some with Platonic undertones: namely, (a) either of two gaits of horses, (b) a thin mass of wind-driven clouds, (c) destruction—as in rack and ruin, (d) to drain from the dregs, as wine or cider, and (e) a wholesale rib cut of lamb between the shoulder and the loin.[25] May's wheeling through "passing rack" takes into her wheeling action a host of other definitions, most of them unkind. Rack is, thus, truly an appropriate word for Beckett's old women. More than the old men who only rack their brains, the old Beckettian women feel their bodies and their souls racked (drawn and quartered, also gaited) while being rocked.

All the homonyms in *Footfalls* and *Rockaby* come to bear upon this key word—"rack." As a frame upon which objects hang, what better way to describe Woman, than as in a rack with chair? What better way to describe May's wheeling than as a racking with her own images? "Rack" also describes May's body which, like hanging meat, appears bloodless, accepting of the ghost. Were it not for doubts that cloud, or wisps of hope, Beckett's women would be objects of flesh, only—impervious to breath or wind.[26] Racks become the rocks upon which female being is founded.

The Demeter myth in Beckett is central to Beckett's coming to terms with the quality of suffering which feminine grief offers the rest of humanity. This quality is different in kind from that of the old man: more in touch with death, it is like a summoning of the seeds of Persephone. To understand the mythic nature of Beckett's imagination is to understand how we must stand under all literate expression, all verbalism, especially those phrases that fly quickly to our lips. We can never communicate clearly, exactly, and precisely. Artists, as Beckett describes them, know this as truth and so engage in new discourse patterns that will let in the dark side. Theirs is a discourse with the objective side of the self, and with objects. Theirs is a dying to old egoistic reflexes. And so the old woman in her rocking chair in *Rockaby*, unlike Murphy in his rocking chair in *Murphy*, is a Beckettian artist. Her companionless condition sets the stage for ventures down into the objective and more poetic self.

6   The Myth of the Eternal Regression

While all of Beckett's characters are compelled to go back or go down, this compulsion takes on special urgency in two recent prose pieces, *Company* and *Ill Seen Ill Said*. The former—what many have called Beckett's autobiography—conveys a deep, drawing power of something other than self-propulsion. Fragments of earlier moments assume a driving importance. Objects, layered with associations of sadness or sweetness, become the things to which the voice cannot help but respond. The narrator feels himself being narrated by a "company" or cast, not all of them human. The latter piece concerns an old woman who leaves her hovel on winter nights when the moon whitens the stones. She is drawn out by the moon, by the stones, where her feet take her to an enchanted zone. There she encounters various others, notably a mysterious unnamed "twelve," a greatcoat, some lambs. She is not the mover of her actions. In both cases what moves the mind or draws the feet is something utterly other than willed volition.

What is it about these ghostly figments that so enthralls Beckett's characters, drawing them back, again and again? This question can be answered by reference to two significant thinkers of our present age whose claim is that modern consciousness is in need of renewal by premodern beliefs which we in our egoism have largely forgotten. Their claims are precisely those of Samuel Beckett. Beckett's mythic imagination, with its "drawing" power, forces us against our wills to feel our souls, really. That Beckett's recent minimalist pieces are fiction expresses an insistence that fiction and reality—or myth and reality—can no longer afford to be separate entities. In fiction Beckett joins the mythmakers, who require that real events be read for their connection with deeper, more interior, time—not the time of mere reality but the time of real time, *in illo tempore*.

Mircea Eliade's several works on premodern consciousness, cited previously, make this point theoretically and historically real. In *Cosmos and History*, Eliade describes the instinct of primitive peoples to "return" periodically to another space, where the self can feel the pulse of humanity of all time and can renew itself. The need to regenerate soul, Eliade says, was also a need to with-

71

draw body. In his *Quest*, he describes how man's too-literal stress on bodied existence had to be destroyed, made to feel victimized, not centered, so as to move consciousness away from its bodied or merely literal perspective. Such a pattern of regression was also followed by religious alchemists, who pummelled physical substances (like lead) in their laboratories to effect an imaginary transformation from their own leaden way of seeing things. Return patterns, Eliade says, allowed initiates to create themselves over again, inside an other, more inclusive cosmos of person, animal, thing.[1]

A second significant thinker of today who can shed light on Beckett's myth of eternal regression (as I call it) is James Hillman, whose work in depth psychology I have also cited previously. Hillman speaks the same language as Beckett. Both insist that the modern soul is endangered by an excessive literalism that has forgotten how to read the world because of a loss of the metaphoric sense. Both insist that the splitting-off of soul from an objective cosmos to a subjective "I," is an egoistic error of dualistic thinking, embraced by Cartesianism, scientism, and positivism. Both suggest ways to heal this collective sickness. In a talk delivered at a conference on postmodernism,[2] Hillman stated that what is needed now is a new/old aestheticism that brings the mathematical (or metaphoric) Forms and the organic (or literal) enactments of these Forms back together again. Plato's *Republic* and early dialogues, of course, separated metaphor from reality, making any as-if reality of Forms an abstract principle perceived only by the rational mind. Metaphoric thinking was thus rationalized, made abstract, and ultimately literalized. But Plato's *Timaeus*—a later Platonic dialogue—serves, for Hillman, as an example of a more appropriate aesthetic for modern lost souls. In this later dialogue Plato envisioned a bringing together of perfect mathematical proportion in animal shapes and in the designs and patterns repeated on animal bodies. Hillman suggests that should we begin to see, in accordance with Plato's teachings, the shapes of our world (animals, objects, images) as Forms living among us, we would begin to acquire the metaphoric sense.

In a recent writing reviewing the field of archetypal psychology, Hillman makes a similar point about how things can animate soul: "The re-animation of things by means of metaphor was already indicated by Vico (S.N. ll, 1.2), who wrote that 'metaphor . . . gives sense and passion to insensate things.' As the metaphorical perspective gives new animation to soul, so too it re-vitalizes areas that had been assumed not ensouled. . . . In this way, the poetic basis of mind (q.v.) takes psychology out of the confines of the laboratory and consulting room . . . into a psychology of things . . . with interiority, things as the display of fantasy."[3]

This last chapter will focus on Beckett's final stage of the Beckettian quest backwards into sensing, where an old woman and an old man return to the child;

that is, to the places of primal imagining. Beckett's myth of the regression goes "far behind the eye" (I, 55), where the first person fades out and the "I" is no longer central. Such a discussion at the end turns us back to beginnings—to cosmos—once infused with meaning but now hardly fathomable. Subjects have lost original power because of a "sterilisation of the living imagination" (PV, 148). But Beckett's mythic writing shows a way in darkness. This is a way of sensing soul in the heart of things.

In *Ill Seen Ill Said* an old woman first is seen in a room stripped of decoration. She spends her time sitting in a chair, lying on a bed, eating from a bowl, looking at a picture album, and going back and forth to a window to gaze at the moon or the stars. Occasionally, she is drawn from her cabin, finding herself among stones. As with Woman in *Rockaby*, things rather than people are her companions. Beckett captures the mystery of this situation through his discourse pattern, which, as Marjorie Perloff has noted, is a battle between pedantry ("Simply note how those still faithful have moved apart" (I, 42) and fairytale ("Still fresh the coffer fiasco what now of all things but a trapdoor" (40).[4]

Indeed, a battle between what the eye sees and what behind-the-eye sees sets a stage for two very different foci. We, as readers, witness constant fade-outs of a scene where someone other than the author controls the camera. Images enter and vanish and reenter from the void. The reader's eye must muster and then turn inward, constantly trying to readjust sense. Diction alternates between poetry and pedantry, between contemporary and ancient word patterns. Verbs drop their auxiliary "is" and "are," become hidden altogether, or delay action until the end of sentences in Germanic fashion. Words echoing other Beckett texts assume charged meaning. Fragments, lacking verbs, pile on top of each other, forcing a different kind of reading. And paragraphs, separated one from another by blank spaces (serving the same dramatic function as, for example, the chime in *Footfalls*), opens us up to total con-fusion: "White walls. High time. White as new. No wind. Not a breath. Unbeaten on by all that comes beating down. And mystery the sun has spared them. The sun that once beat down. So east and west sides the required clash. South gable no problem. But the other. That door. Careful" (I, 42–43).

Beckett's urging into space, not time, is like a primitive ritual pattern. The ritual takes us into a vertical dimension where "—ing" returns to the senses: hovering, menacing, shivering, threatening, weeping, lowering, tightening, loosening. What, as readers, are we? Where, as voyagers, are we? Sensing can be dangerous, for to bring back object power could be to re-place the "I."

The old woman's ability to see ill and say ill—what others might call an inability or a sickness—nevertheless endows objects with senses. She goes with what little she knows: "Suffice to watch the grass. How motionless it droops. Till under the relentless eye it shivers. With faintest shiver from its innermost"

(I, 29). The woman's "relentless eye" does not yield clear, scientific data concerning a blade of grass. Even so, it seems to see into the very core of the blade's center. This act of nonscientific seeing causes a real effect—the object's shivering. One could, of course, say that such shivering is merely a sign of protoplasm, alive but inert. But in terms of the text, "shivering" seems much more a reaction of one eye penetrating another eye, quickening it. In terms of the context of Beckett's work, such eyeing recalls *Rockaby*'s Woman, who seeks more from objects, since subjects give her less.

Other contexts embedded here suggest a myth that lies deep within Beckett's old women; namely, the myth of Demeter. Helios, the sun who oversees all, had the only eye that saw what happened to Persephone. Mythically, the eye that sees is truly ambivalent; for Helios saw the rape and yet he shined on, refused to tell. To "know happiness," as the previous chapter suggested, is to come to terms with the the void, No. But to "see," as this chapter will suggest, is to see with lidded eyes—more than one can tell.

Demeter's *mythos* makes a claim in the text of *Ill Seen Ill Said* in ways that recall *Not I.* Both texts take us to where we are "dazed" by what we see in the day. As in *Not I,* Persephone motifs in *Ill Seen Ill Said* contain references to *grassy meadow*, found in Beckett's phrase "meagre pastures," "rankest weed," "clover" (8), "moor" with "lambs" and "ewes" (11), "pastures" (13, 24, 28, 30, 41, 44), "withered flowers" (15), "pastures far from shelter" (15). These references continue in the *suddenness* of the rape event, found in Beckett's phrases "culprit," "demolition" (9), "suddenly come . . . suddenly gone" (10), "But quick seize her where she is best to be seized" (15), "Quick seeing" (15), "suddenly no longer there" (17, 52), "Suddenly open. A flash. The suddenness of all!" (19), "Pfft occulted" (20), "Quick the eyes" (39), "Quick say" (54), "Quick find her again" (54), "Quick say it suddenly can and farewell say say farewell" (59); and a reference to the *scream,* as in Beckett's words "Silence at the eye of the scream" (29). Unlike *Not I* references to rape, or masturbation, in this text are either stated or implied: "pubis intertwined" (31), "body that scandal" (32), "sole hands" (32), "sole pubis" (32), "spell unbinding" (32), "On and on they keep" (32), "Rhythm of a labouring heart" (32), "Within an ace of the crotch" (32), "clad flesh" (32), "Throughout this confrontation the sun stands still. That is to say the earth. Not to recoil on until the parting" (45), "Unlikely site of olden kisses given and received" (49).

Demeter motifs include references to *constant walking* as in Beckett's phrases "She is drawn to a certain spot" (11), "she must to it" (12), "to her feet the prayer, Take her" (12), "going out or coming in" (13), "crossing the threshold both ways" (13), "At one or the other window" (14), "faint comings and goings" (14), "She is there. Again." (19), "All in black she comes and goes" (21), "she reappears" (24), "Back and forth" (30), "Hither and thither toward the stones" (36), "She reemerges on her back" (38), "She reappears at evening" (46). These motifs continue in references to *anguish*, as in Beckett's mention of "No trace of frolic" (11), "Rapt before the sky" (14), "No more!" (15), "the desert eye fills with tears" (17), "Imagination at wit's ends spreads its sad wings" (17), "Tears" (17, 18, 25), "Weeping over weeping" (18), "some ancient horror" (29), "filthy eye of flesh" (30), "the howls of laughter of the damned" (54). Then, there are the references to *dress* as in Beckett's descriptions "black skirt" (21), "her long black shadow" (24), "weeds' mock calm" (30), "lace at the wrists" (31), "She on the contrary immaculately black" (33), "long black skirt" (42). There is also reference to *Demeter's candelabrum*, as in Beckett's "a candle or two" (24); and, also, references to *sitting, staring*, as found in Beckett's phrase "sits as though turned to stone" (7), "she freezes" (7), "Riveted to some detail" (17), "rigid Memnon pose" (35). Further dynamics of the Demeter *mythos* are found in *winter-spring* images, as in mention of crocus (10, 29), winter (15, 33), snow (15, 33) and in phrases like "At crocus time it would be making for the distant tomb" (16), "Winter evening" (22, 44), "Winter night" (41, 45), "endless winter" (50), "One April afternoon" (57); as well as the specific Demeter mythologem of *dry streams*, with such phrases as "The feeling at times of being below sea level" (9), "entire surface under grass" (10).[5]

The eye of the old woman seems curiously like a dry stream itself. "Gaping pupil thinly nimbed with washen blue. No trace of humour. None any more. Unseeing. As if dazed by what seen behind the lids" (I, 39). This eye is like Holloway's eye in the story Henry tells, in *Embers*. But unlike Holloway's, this eye does not simply fill with tears; it plumbs its own depths. The "humourless eye" finds landscapes and meanings not in daylight but in dark, not on surfaces but buried within, and not in the human sphere, but in objects. A first or primal nature returns to the old woman in her evident distress and abandonment. It is then, as Beckett pointed out in *Proust*, that reality is felt most cruelly. And it is also then and then only, he insisted, that the object may enchant (P, 11).

Fifty years after he wrote that treatise on things (*Proust*), Beckett gave this example of an object besieged with its own mystery in *Ill Seen Ill Said*:

> Of tarnished silver pisciform it hangs by its hook from a nail. It trembles faintly without cease. As if here without cease the earth faintly quaked. The oval handle is wrought to a semblance of scales. The shank a little bent leads up to the hook the eye so far still dry. A lifetime of hooking has lessened its curvature. To the point at certain moments of its seeming unfit for service. Child's play with a pliers to restore it. Was there once a time she did? (I, 18)

Here, a boot hook is more than itself. The hook's "pisciform" or fish shape suggests a "semblance of scales" made from an oval handle that sets It apart from the familiar world of mere seeing or mere object-ism into a world charged with meaning. Released from its utilitarian function as boot hook—that which buttons up—it assumes richer, more primitive associations: fish with Christ; hook and nail with crucifixion; earthquake that opened a spiritual journey from *purgatorio* to *paradisio*. Beckett's twisting logic makes us wonder whether child's play can restore Christ's suffering, whether suffering can reanimate soul, or whether con-fusing Christian and Greek *mythos* in an old wives' tale can bind religion backwards (*re-ligio*) to myth. These are some of the enchantments the old woman's "humourless eye" sees in a thing flooded with sense. These are moments of sensing "the Paradise that has been lost" (P, 55).

Company, Beckett's most child-centered fictional work, is narrated by an old man. Alone, the narrator lies in a dark room with no one to keep him company but the disembodied "one" of the narrative voice. To Beckett audiences the technique is familiar. By telling stories "one" transcends time and place. An old man can turn himself into a boy, a solitary child, even into children. But "one" is also locked into feeling, for "one" at whatever end of the time continuum constantly feels existentially alone, abandoned, forsaken, inside a universe where the gods no longer speak. To transform this feeling, "one" must imagine. By telling fragments of stories "one" can re-member the present situation—give it body or texture, put its parts together differently inside another text. Each sad fragment of story or figment of memory deepens the present time like layers of a hive, until "one" becomes cocooned inside tissues of fear, loneliness, or shame. "One" becomes more-than-one.

Beckett presents this preconscious world of the old man variously. One way is to suggest that the old man's falls are basic regressions to childlike crawls: "So as he crawls the mute count. Grain by grain in the mind. One two three four one. Knee hand knee hand two. One foot. Till say five he falls. Then sooner or later on from naught anew. One two three four one. Knee hand knee hand two. Six. So on. In what he wills a beeline" (C, 49). This passage, with its total concentration on simple movement, captures the essence of the child. Movement becomes a total act, both of body (engaging all fours, knee with hand) and of mind (mute counting). An inability to establish any clear line of direction indicates a childlike lack of coordination between how one graphs what one wills with the mind and what the body does anyway, mindlessly. Minute actions, failing to yield larger significance, seem to be merely single "one's" of getting up and going on after falling down. The beeline wills the way.

We are reminded here of Moran's journey back, in *Molloy*, launching his body across muddy solitudes. His journey home—during which he experiences failing flesh, dulled habits, and a general metamorphosis into mindless thought (M, 166–68), is also a mythic regressing into primal sensing. He, too, counts his steps: "That night I set out for home. I did not get far. But it was a start. It is

the first step that counts. The second counts less" (165). Like the old man narrator in *Company*, Moran moves less with clock time and more with primal time,
especially as he nears home. And, also like the narrator of *Company*, Moran's
regression is signalled by a fascination with tiny things, such as flies (M, 166)
and bees (168–69). Observing the return of bees to their hive, Moran describes
their every minute action, even their hummings, in a way that could describe all
basic Beckettian return patterns—as a "dance" between mathematical (or metaphoric) and organic (or literal) functions. To be willed as the bees are willed is
to repeat same patterns on multiply different levels.[6]

Another way Beckett presents the preconscious world of the old man in
Company is through a combative tone, now masculine, now feminine, each bat-
tling for center stage. One tone, masculine, is beaconlike in its attempt to pin-
point truths, verify events, and describe particulars. Its function is to circum-
scribe feeling by capturing it in a literal place that can be named. Language that
pinpoints, however, is really only words "about." In this sense words prevent
sensing by their determination to maintain bodied truth and placed event in
merely present time: "See hearer clearer. Which of all the ways of lying supine
the least likely in the long run to pall? After long straining eyes closed prone in
the dark the following. But first naked or covered? If only with a sheet. Naked.
Ghostly in the voice's glimmer that bonewhite flesh for company. Head resting
mainly on occipital bump aforesaid. Legs joined at attention. Feet splayed
ninety degrees" (C, 56–57). Questions are asked for answers, precisely, with
emphasis placed on numeral exactitude. Circumscribing the situation in such a
manner yields nothing less than naked absurdity.

The other tone in *Company* is feminine and is flowing rather than flat. Its
function is to connect the narrator with feeling, not fact—with the color and
texture of an event. Such a tone opens the self to its primal depths, where primitive tides flourish: "A faint voice at loudest. It slowly ebbs till almost out of hearing. Then slowly back to faint full. At each slow ebb hope slowly dawns that it is
dying. He must know it will flow again" (C, 17). This voice, faint and then loud,
"dawns" inside the speaker's mind and mimes nature. It is like Molloy "who himself is night, day and night" (M, 67)—the same but different, paddling with an
old bit of driftwood (69). Such a voyage of tides and times places the ego where
it cannot make sense of presentiment. Such a tone re-places the notion of how
one sees, what one sees, and where one sees, to a place that is both older and
younger than any definition would allow.

A third way Beckett suggests the child alive in the old man's consciousness
is by déjà vu technique. As readers reading this text, we are thrust back to earlier
Beckett texts that haunt our reading. Beckett's deconstruction of every constructed meaning puts us in a different relation to text. We can not master these
words because of a tendency the words have to resist our efforts to define or cate-

gorize.[7] Instead, we are thrust into the middle of worded situations that bring memory back into mind.

A small boy's fascination with the sky, for example, places *Company* among earlier Beckett texts, one text deconstructing another: "Looking up at the blue sky and then at your mother's face you break the silence asking her if it is not in reality much more distant than it appears. The sky that is. The blue sky" (C, 10–11). This particular hearkening back is repeated twice more in *Company*: once when the small boy climbs a tree in order to get nearer the sky, straining to see the blue (25); a second time when the boy, now young man, sees an eternity of blue sky in the eyes of his lover (40). What the eyes ache to see cannot possibly be attained on earth. A juxtaposition of times, a confusion of sky with mother's face and then with lover's eyes, a yearning for closeness with objects that are distant, beyond reach—all imply a mode of seeing that deepens sensing.

"The End," a short story written thirty years before *Company*, presents the same situation of an old man remembering his youth. Juxtaposing a child's wonder at the mysteries of creation with a mother's profanity, Beckett juxtaposes as well the two zones of child and adult, sacred and profane. The early story places this juxtaposition crudely: "A small boy, stretching out his hands and looking up at the blue sky, asked his mother how such a thing was possible. Fuck off she said" (E, 50). Later in the story the old man meditates upon the sky in ways that recall his earlier, childlike self: "Most of the time I looked up at the sky, but without focussing it, for why focus it? Most of the time it was a mixture of white, blue, and grey, and then at evening all the evening colours. I felt it weighing softly on my face" (E, 64). This meditation is similar to the predicament of young Krapp in *Krapp's Last Tape*, seeking the sky in his lover's eyes (K, 27). To connect sky and eyes, against such a context of texts, is to connect the sacred with the profane. Krapp's plea to his lover to be "let in" seems more a plea to reunite with a sacred dimension of the sky (mirrored by the eyes) than to be let in to her physical body. Such a quest of Krapp is but another instance of male seeking by Beckett's "one." All of these singular seekings fail, utterly, on a literal level when the quester asks his question. But on a deeper level, rebuffs by the mother image and non-answers from feminine figures form a pattern. Living on in memory, this pattern of rebuff has the power to transpose "one" into "company"—the material of an ongoing, creative *récit* that no single paradigm can determine or arrest.[8]

The effect these superimpositions create is to place the ego differently in the cosmos of the self. The ego loses its center and "I" yields to "he," "she," "you," or "it," where soul is always found.[9] The child, like the old man and the old woman, lives more truly "behind the eye" as a spectator rather than actor. The head in which the child is becomes, thus, a sea of relationships among humans, animals, and nature. Language, too, takes on flux. For instance, "shed," "rail," and "slip" are the nouns most often used in *That Time* and recall key things of the old man's past. But they are also verbs of felt experience: "to shed," "to rail," and "to slip" describe the anguish a child feels weeping, cursing, and hiding.

Remembered as naughty, a constant seeker after his parents' affection, the child in *Company* simply wants to be a brave boy for his father and a good boy for his mother. But on the other hand he yearns for broader vistas—the sky or the sea—that can take him away from his literal biological roots in the West, in Ireland. In perhaps the most poignant passage in *Company*, meanings converge around the words "sere" and "box" (the boy is a boxed-in seer). These words echo with the repeated word "path" and resound in the rhyme "hedgehog-edging." The passage recalls a moment when the boy finds a hedgehog, feeds it, and puts it in an old hatbox: "Kneeling at your bedside you included it the hedgehog in your detailed prayer to God to bless all you loved. And tossing in your warm bed waiting for sleep to come you were still faintly glowing at the thought of what a fortunate hedgehog it was to have crossed your path as it did. A narrow clay path edged with sere box edging" (C, 30).

Weeks later the boy who had played God to the hedgehog finds it dead: "You are on your back in the dark and have never forgotten what you found then. The mush. The stench" (31). In these regressions, "one" experiences again, all over again, the anguish of former times. "One" is sensing as never before, seeing as never before, able perhaps to become a seer. The last moment in the myth of the eternal regression, sensing, is thus the moment when Beckett's "new mythological reality" (PV, 149) can be seen, felt, and heard—by characters, by auditors, by readers. Let us, then, look at four properties which describe sensing in ways that bring the "Poetry Is Vertical" manifesto of 1932 back to life.

First, we see a new understanding of person or character. To be human, for Beckett, is to lose ego and all of ego's demand for first person singular status. Characters are unnamed, or reduced to initials (H, M, and W in *Company*, for instance) because Beckett is not concerned with specific individual cases. The old man and old woman, like the child, are archetypes which—instead of representing unique references—are, according to Jung, "the formulated resultants of countless typical experiences of our ancestors. . . . the psychic residue of numberless experiences of the same type." In *Company* the narrator is ancestrally primordial—old but young—in ways that convey the archetypal child as Jung described it: "the mythological idea of the child is emphatically not a copy of the empirical child but a symbol clearly recognized as such: It is a wonder-child, a divine child, begotten, born, and brought up in quite extraordinary circumstances, and not—this is the point—a human child. Its deeds are as miraculous or monstrous as its nature and physical condition."[10] With the notion of character as archetype, Beckett forces us to feel being as something we live from and in, no matter how ego would have it. We must learn to let this being be, so that memories can acquire deeper residue.

A second property of sensing, which is also part of a new mythological reality, is Beckett's emphasis on time and place as fluid, not fixed. The here and now reality of history or biography is not only discounted in Beckett's work but mercilessly mocked. Moran in *Molloy* or the narrator of *Company*, attempting to nail events and record body postures by precise angle or degree, shows just how split off the modern mind-body is from its soul-body. This is a post-Cartesian dilemma that Beckett addresses by describing a need to sense time and space, body and mind, in different, transpersonal contexts.

The Japanese have an understanding of this idea. According to Yasunari Takahashi, a Noh play typically starts at the point where everything has already happened. What an audience sees on stage is not the action in the process of its happening, but the arrival of someone else: an other, a ghost from the past.[11] Such a reversal of time and place accomplishes a miracle. An audience situated in present time is placed at once in past time. Historicism is immediately wiped away. When the other arrives, the audience greets it as a part of themselves, buried under the deepest layers of culture—not particularly nor necessarily Japanese (73). Theater becomes a sensing of the space that runs through time.

A third property of this new mythological reality is new language. Dance, music, the rhythm and sounding of words create an opening for an other speaking to come forth. Text linearly ordered must be fragmented, broken, to allow metaphors and images space to speak to the senses. Basic patterns, like paced footfalls; archaic words, like "sere" and "washen"; syntax lapses; the use of chimes; homonyms, like "in thrall"—Beckett's minimalism returns us to zero where all becomes possible.

To find the space and place of new speaking, a mythic poetic should neither succumb to nor resist that which is totally opposite to known experience. Opposition gives energy that enlivens sensing. As the phenomenological philosopher Merleau-Ponty points out, a true artist loves what cannot be known and seeks to be connected with all disjoining forces of being: "The words most charged with philosophy are not necessarily those that contain what they say, but rather those that most energetically open upon Being, because they more closely convey the life of the whole and make our habitual evidences vibrate until they disjoin."[12]

Jung made a similar observation concerning archetypes. Arising from unconsciousness, archetypes express an other reality which interrupts habit and consciousness. To "sense" this other speaking—really the personae of the gods and goddesses—requires a premodern mind in tune with "the forgotten language of the instincts."[13] When the presence of something older is more deeply felt, heard, seen, then and only then can soul-speaking "make" sense.

A language of gesture in Beckett's work also expresses what words cannot tell. In Come and Go three women dressed identically with long coats and wide brimmed hats are seated on a bench surrounded by darkness. Although the stage directions make it clear that none of the women wears a ring, one of the women says that she can "feel the rings" (C & G, 69). The comment is ominous, for each woman has whispered a secret about the others and the others know a secret about her. But what "rings" the women together even more than their whispered secrets is their manner of holding hands: the one on the left holds both right hands, the one in the center holds a right and a left, and the one on the right holds the left hand of each of the others. As Lois More Overbeck points out, this stylized linking of hands forms an image of a möbius strip, or three dimensional sign for infinity.[14] The three appear forever united inside shared memories and unshared secrets—inside the heart of contradiction. The handclasping gesture, because of its three dimensional aspect (where there is neither inside nor outside and where sameness is wrapped inside infinite difference) is Beckett's move away from mere oppositionalism toward a more complicated notion of duality.

Similarly, Beckett's plays Quad I and II illuminate aspects of ritualized drama that have recently been adapted by Western directors to suggest a fusing of elements of Buddhist chanting, martial art forms, poetry, and shaministic practices. Another way of viewing Beckett's dance plays, like Footfalls, What Where, and the Quad plays, is to see them bodying language into sensory dimension. Words like "rack" in Footfalls or phrases like "the works" in What Where imply torture to the body. But the actors' movements, particularly in Footfalls, give more a sense of exquisite anguish. This is in keeping with "rack," defined earlier in chapter 5, as "a toothed bar that meshes with another toothed structure, such as a pinion or gearwheel." It is the meshing that interests. For in bringing together the straight line of the bar with the circle of the gearwheel, a union of opposites is created. This perfect design tortures body. But the play illuminates soul, tortured in perfectly exquisite ways—ways that enthrall us while they hold us in thrall.

Such playing with negation, a continual theme in Beckett's work, has increasingly become a topic of interest to Beckettian critics and directors. The late Richard Ellman, in a beautiful tribute entitled "Samuel Beckett: Nayman of Noland," has this to say about Beckett's naysaying: "Beckett could claim to have given a voice to the third of every existence likely to be spent in decay. His studied reticence about his purpose is justified. To explain is to attenuate. As his writings have become shorter, he has seemed to imply that faithful images of life have to be squeezed out. Yet his musical cadences, his wrought and precise sentences, cannot help but stave off the void."[15] And director (also actor) Pierre Chabert has commented that Beckett's variations in punctuation, rhythm, and voice give the word "No," in *Krapp's Last Tape*, three distinctly different intonations. The effect, Chabert says, is to produce a kind of "verbal ballet."[16]

Finally, Beckett's questing pattern takes those of us stuck in Western Cartesian dualism into new, sensory directions: to the East, where Japanese theater welcomes Beckett's theater home; to mysticism, where lips and eyes remain closed and articulation is impossible; to the "No," where the only possible way of communicating is to reach into stillness after the words are still. And surely there is a special affinity Beckett's works share with the night. For there, as he says in *Proust*, human banality is transformed and solid objects decompose (34). In decomposition hard things become moist. But in that process something else is going on. Perhaps this decomposing takes our Western eyes and ears into keener tones—those less attuned to literalism. As Beckett shows with Molloy, in the night during decomposition we awaken: "And that night there was no question of moon, nor any other light, but it was a night of listening, a night given to the faint soughing and sighing stirring at night in little pleasure gardens" (M, 48).

Notes

Introduction

1. For critical writings on Beckett's philosophy see, for instance, Sighle Kennedy, *Murphy's Bed: A Study of Real Sources and Sur-real Associations in Samuel Beckett's First Novel* (Lewisburg, Pa.: Bucknell University Press, 1971); Edith Kern, *Existential Thought and Fictional Technique: Kierkegaard, Sartre, Beckett* (New Haven, Conn.: Yale University Press, 1972); Rubin Rabinovitz, "Watt from Descartes to Schopenhaur," in *Modern Irish Literature: Essays in Honor of William York Tyndall*, eds. James D. Brophy and Raymond J. Porter (Wooster, Ohio: Iona Press, 1972); Steven J. Rosen, *Samuel Beckett and the Pessimistic Tradition* (New Brunswick, N.J.: Rutgers University Press, 1976). For critical writings on Beckett's aesthetics see Stanley E. Gray, "Beckett and Queneau as Formalists," *James Joyce Quarterly* 8, no. 4 (Summer 1971):392–402; H. Porter Abbott, *The Fiction of Samuel Beckett: Form and Effect* (Berkeley, Calif.: University of California Press, 1973); Frederick Busi, *The Transformations of Godot* (Lexington, Ky.: University Press of Kentucky, 1980); David H. Hesla, *The Shape of Chaos: An Interpretation of the Art of Samuel Beckett* (Minneapolis, Minn.: The University of Minnesota Press, 1971); Melvin J. Friedman, ed. *Samuel Beckett Now: Critical Approaches to His Novels, Poetry and Plays* (Chicago: University of Chicago Press, 1970). For critical writings on Beckett and deconstruction theory, see Herbert Blau, *The Impossible Theater: A Manifesto* (New York: Macmillan, 1961) and his *The Eye of the Prey: Subversions of the Postmodern* (Bloomington, Ind.: Indiana University Press, 1987).

2. See, for instance, Susan Brienza, *Samuel Beckett's New Worlds: Styles of Metafiction* (Norman, Okla.: Oklahoma University Press, 1987); S. E. Gontarski, *Happy Days: A Manuscript Study* (Columbus, Ohio: Ohio State University Libraries, 1977); Inger Christensen, *The Meaning of Metafiction: A Critical Study of Selected Novels by Sterne, Nabokov, Barth and Beckett* (New York: Columbia University Press, 1981).

3. See Curtis M. Brooks, "The Mythic Pattern in Waiting for Godot," *Modern Drama* 9 (1966):292–99; Edith Kern, "Moran-Molloy: The Hero as Author," *Perspective* 11, no. 3 (Autumn 1959):183–93; Vivian Mercier, "Samuel Beckett and the Sheela-Na-Gig," *Kenyon Review* 23, no. 2 (Spring 1961):299–328; Rubin Rabinovitz, "Molloy and the Archetypal Traveller," *Journal of Beckett Studies* no. 5 (Autumn 1979):25–44; Katherine H. Burkman, "Initiation Rites in Samuel Beckett's *Waiting for Godot*," *Papers in Comparative Studies* 3 (1984):137–52; also Katherine H. Burkman, ed. *Myth and Ritual in the Plays of Samuel Beckett* (Cranbury, N.J.: Fairleigh Dickinson Press, 1987). Other critics have made passing mention of Beckett's use of myth, notably Breon Mitchell, "The Manuscript Stages of Beckett's *Come and Go*," *Modern Drama* 19 no. 3 (September 1976):245–54, in which reference is made to the three women as the three Graces; Katherine Kelly, "The Orphic Mouth in *Not I*," *Journal of Beckett Studies* no. 6 (Autumn 1980):73–80, which explores the myth of Orpheus; and Gabor Mihalyi, "Beckett's *Godot* and the Myth of Alienation," *Modern Drama* 9 (December 1966), which takes myth from a philosophic perspective. Other writings approach Beck-

ett through Jungian psychology, notably: Eva Metman, "Reflections on Samuel Beckett's Plays," in *Samuel Beckett: A Collection of Critical Essays*, Martin Esslin, ed. (Englewood Cliffs, N.J.: Prentice-Hall, Inc., 1965); and J. D. O'Hara, "Jung and the Narratives of *Molloy,*" *Journal of Beckett Studies* no. 7 (Spring 1982):19–48. These papers, however, do not relate the Jungian understanding to Beckett's mythic imagination.

4. See Tom Moore, *Rituals of the Imagination* (Dallas, Tex.: The Pegasus Foundation, 1983), 20–21.

5. C. G. Jung, *The Undiscovered Self*, trans. R. F. C. Hull (Boston, Mass.: Little, Brown & Co., 1958), 96.

6. Knowing the dark, or seeing the shadow, is a significant but little acknowledged idea phrased by Beckett in his own critical writings. A Jungian notion of "shadow" with its importance for the discovery of selfhood can be seen in Beckett's writing in "Peintres de l'empêchement," *Derrière le Miroir*, Nos. 11 and 12 (June 1948):3, 4, 7, where he compares seeing into the night as seeing into an entire universe. See Lawrence Harvey, *Samuel Beckett: The Poet and Critic* (Princeton, N.J.: Princeton University Press 1970), 427. Compare Beckett's phrasing with that of Jung: "we carry in ourselves a real shadow whose existence is grounded in our instinctual nature. The dynamism and imagery of the instincts together form an *à priori* which no man can overlook without the gravest risk to himself" (*The Undiscovered Self*, 83).

7. S. E. Gontarski, *The Intent of Undoing in Samuel Beckett's Dramatic Texts* (Bloomington, Ind.: Indiana University Press, 1985).

8. J. Hillis Miller, "The Critic as Host," in *Deconstruction and Criticism* (New York: Continuum Pub. Co., 1979), 251.

9. Rubin Rabinovitz, "Repetition and Underlying Meanings in Samuel Beckett's Trilogy," Keynote address presented at the International Samuel Beckett Conference, University of Stirling, Scotland (12 August 1986).

10. S. E. Gontarski, "The World Première of *Ohio Impromptu,*" *Journal of Beckett Studies*, no. 8 (Autumn 1982):133.

11. Brienza, "Perilous Journeys on Beckett's Stages: Travelling Through Words," in *Myth and Ritual*, 46.

12. Of the two levels of literalism, one level is that of real, denotative representations: the level of literal one-to-one correspondence; a second level of literalism is metaphoric and is suggestive or connotative rather than representative. Beckett's word plays often involve both levels at once, such that a term may be heard on two, sometimes contradictory, levels—confounding the first level of literal meaning by introducing the second level of metaphoric meaning, implying thereby multiple meanings within single utterances.

13. For more on the word "rack" and its special uses in Beckett's work, see subsequent chapters, especially chapter 5, note 25.

1 — A Poetics of Myth

1. Clive Bell, as chief spokesman for the Bloomsbury group, articulated an aesthetic totally opposite from that of Beckett. For Bell, art is cleanly separated from everyday life and provides a spiritual experience, which he describes as "the thrilling raptures of those who have climbed the cold, white peaks of art." *Aesthetics and Post-Impressionism: A New Theory of Art* (London: Chatto and Windus, 1949), 33.

2. Gontarski, *The Intent of Undoing*, compares Beckett's aesthetics to gambling by the phrase "aleatory aesthetics." Unpredictability, as a "chaotic system" in nature, is also the subject of

Ilya Prigogine's scientific study. See Ilya Prigogine and Isabelle Stengers, *Order Out of Chaos* (New York: Bantam Books, 1984). For a discussion of Beckett's "poetics of indigence" see James Knowlson and John Pilling, *Frescoes of the Skull: The Later Prose and Drama of Samuel Beckett.* London: John Calder Ltd., 1979.

3. Beckett puns on how that which is out of the ordinary puts one in better touch with a different kind of hearing sensation. Of Denis Devlin's poems he says, "the insistence with which the ground invades the surface throughout [the poem "Intercessions"] is quite extraordinary. Extra-audenary" (D, 293).

4. Molloy's sympathy with all of nature is like Jung's description of the collective unconscious which is "as wide as the world and open to all the world. There (one feels) I am the object of every subject . . . utterly at one with the world." (*Collected Works* of C. G. Jung. Vol. 9, pt. 1, *The Archetypes and the Collective Unconscious* [hereafter cited CW], trans. R. F. C. Hull [Princeton, N.J.: Princeton University Press, 1968], 22). It is also like the meditation of Giordano Bruno, whom Beckett placed in a tradition with Vico and Joyce. Bruno's "Egyptian Reflection," like Molloy's soliloquy, was: "Draw into yourself all sensations of everything created, fire and water, dry and moist, imagining that you are everywhere, on earth, in the sea, in the sky, that you are not yet born, in the maternal womb, adolescent, old, dead, beyond death." (Frances A. Yates, *Giordano Bruno and the Hermetic Tradition* [London: Routledge & Kegan Paul, 1964], 31–32).

5. Deirdre Bair, *Samuel Beckett: A Biography* (New York: Harcourt, Brace, Jovanovich, 1978), 457.

6. Jung, "Ulysses: A Monologue," in CW 15, *The Spirit in Man, Art, and Literature,* 109–35.

7. Gontarski is the only critic I know of who also draws attention to the Jung-Beckett overlap in the pages of *transition* 19/20 (1930). See his *Intent of Undoing,* xiii.

8. Jung, "The Tavistock Lectures, Lecture 3" in CW 18, *The Symbolic Life* (1978), 73.

9. See also Lawrence Harvey, *Samuel Beckett: Poet and Critic* (Princeton: Princeton University Press, 1970), 435, for an interpretation of Beckett's "new thing" art must do as a letting-in of being. The phrase "new mythological reality" occurs in the "Poetry Is Vertical" manifesto signed by Beckett and others (*transition* 21 [March 1932]:148–49). And see also Beckett, "Denis Devlin," 293: "It is naturally in the image that this profound and abstruse self-consciousness first emerges."

10. Beckett wrote of Bram van Velde's work: "C'est la chose seule, isolèe par le besoin de la voir, par le besoin de voir. La chose immobile dans le vide, voilà enfin la chose visible, l'objet pûr" ("It is the thing itself, isolated by a need to be seen, by a need to see. The thing fixed in emptiness, there finally as a visible thing, a pure object"—translation mine. ("La Peinture des van Velde, ou: le monde et le pantalon," in *Les cahiers d'art [1945–46]:*356). This idea of the object's need and inner reality was repeated in Beckett's "Hommage à Jack B. Yeats," *Les lettres nouvelles* 2 (April 1954): 619–20.

11. Maurice Merleau-Ponty, *The Visible and the Invisible,* trans. Alphonso Lingis, ed. Claude Lefort (Evanston, Ill.: Northwestern University Press, 1968), 198.

12. See Charles Boer, "Poetry and Psyche," *Spring: An Annual of Archetypal Psychology and Jungian Thought* (1979):99 (Hereafter cited as *Spring*).

13. See Niel Micklem, "The Intolerable Image: The Mythic Background of Psychosis," *Spring* (1979):1–19, for a radical approach to imagery.

14. See *The Analects of Confucius,* trans. Arthur Waley (London: G. Allen & Union Ltd., 1949).

15. As Beckett says, "Un dévoilement sans fin, voile derrière voile, plan sur plan de transparences imparfaites, un dévoilement vers l'indévoilable, le rien, la chose à nouveau" (an endless unveiling, veil after veil, the imperfect transparencies of superimposing planes, an unveiling towards that which cannot be unveiled) trans. Mme. Melzer. See Harvey, *Samuel Beckett,* 426. Compare

Beckett's notion of unveiling with that of Jung, who, in writing on Joyce's Ulysses, says, "when something is 'symbolic,' it means that a person divines its hidden, ungraspable nature and is trying desperately to capture in words the secret that eludes him. Whether it is something of the world he is trying to grasp or something of the spirit, he must turn to it with all his mental powers and penetrate all its iridescent veils in order to bring to the light of day the gold that lies jealously hidden in the depths. But the shattering thing about *Ulysses* is that behind the thousand veils nothing lies hidden" (CW 15, 123–24).

16. Rosemary Pountney, "On Acting Mouth in *Not I*," *Journal of Beckett Studies* no. 1 (Winter 1976):84.

17. Whitelaw's comments, together with Beckett's words to Whitelaw, are cited in Bair, *Samuel Beckett*, 625.

18. Charles Olson's scorn of ego psychology is amazingly like Beckett's. See Olson, "Proprioception," in *Charles Olson: Additional Prose*, ed. George Butterick (Bolinas, Calif.: Four Seasons Press, 1974):17. In this prose piece Olson disdains social life as mere surface, no flow, and ego as needing to be washed out.

19. Translation mine. Beckett's original is "on commence enfin à voir, dans le noir. Dans le noir qui est aube et midi et soir et nuit d'un ciel vide, d'une terre fixe." See Harvey, *Samuel Beckett*, 427.

20. See Owen Barfield, "The Meaning of the Word 'Literal,' " in *Metaphor and Symbol*, eds. L. C. Knights and B. Cottle (London: Butterworths), 1960; Philip Wheelwright, *Metaphor and Reality* (Bloomington, Ind.: Indiana University Press, 1968); and Jung, in CW 9, 1, *The Archetypes and the Collective Unconscious*.

21. See Bair, *Samuel Beckett*, Preface, and compare with Jung, "Psychology and Poetry" reprinted as "Psychology and Literature" (1930), in CW 15, 84–108.

2 — The Myth of the Non-Hero: Moran

1. Joseph Campbell, *The Hero with a Thousand Faces* (Cleveland, Ohio: World Publishing Co., 1949), 39–40.

2. Albert Camus, *The Myth of Sisyphus*, trans. Justin O'Brien (New York: Alfred A. Knopf, 1955), 64; and Albert Camus, *The Plague*, trans. Gilbert Stuart (New York: Random House, 1969).

3. In an interview with Tom Driver Beckett said the following concerning the relation between art and life: "The confusion is not my invention. The only chance of renovation is to open our eyes and see the mess. It is not a mess you can make sense of." In "Beckett by the Madeleine," *Columbia University Forum* 4 (Summer 1961):21–25.

4. Edith Kern, "Moran-Molloy: The Hero as Author," *Perspective* 11 (Autumn 1959):184. For other critical writings on Molloy as hero, see also Rubin Rabinovitz, "*Molloy* and the Archetypal Traveller," *Journal of Beckett Studies* no. 5 (Autumn 1979):25–44; Ruby Cohn, *Back to Beckett* (Princeton, N.J.: Princeton University Press, 1973), 83; and David Hesla, *The Shape of Chaos* (Minneapolis, Minn.: University of Minnesota Press, 1971).

5. Robert Scholes, "The Fictional Criticism of the Future," *Triquarterly* 34 (Fall 1975):237.

6. H. Porter Abbott, *The Fiction of Samuel Beckett: Form and Effect* (Berkeley, Calif.: University of California Press, 1973), 99, 114.

7. Inger Christensen, *The Meaning of Metafiction: A Critical Study of Selected Novels by Sterne, Nabokov, Barth and Beckett* (New York: Columbia University Press, 1981), 113–15.

8. Hesla, *Shape*, 50.

9. James Eliopolos, *Samuel Beckett's Dramatic Language* (Mouton Publishing Co., 1975), 72. See also Rubin Rabinovitz's keynote address "Repetition" to the Beckett conference at the University of Stirling. In this address, Rabinovitz made a slightly different point from that of Eliopolos, more akin with the thrust of my argument; namely, that Beckett's repetitions debunk traditional forms and shatter the hero concept.

10. Mercier, *Beckett*, 51.

11. Jung, "The Tavistock Lectures, Lecture 3 (1935)," in CW 18, *The Symbolic Life* (1978), 93.

12. According to ancient belief, the knee—not the womb—was source of generation, as evidenced by the Indo-European group of languages that has for the word "knee" terms often interchangeable with generation (Irish, *glun*: Latin, *genu*). See R. B. Onians, *Origins of European Thought* (Cambridge: Cambridge University Press, 1954), 174.

13. According to Jung the left-hand path does not lead upward into the kingdom of eternal ideas but downward into nature, particularly into the bestial, instinctual foundations of natural human existence, where soul lives. See CW 12, *Psychology and Alchemy* (1968), 205. In Dante's *Inferno* it is the lower foot, *pie fermo sepre era 'l piu basso* ("the firm foot was always the lower") that is kept firm because the upper or right foot in its weakened state needed to make the journey down to meet the beast. See *The Divine Comedy of Dante Alighieri*, trans. John D. Sinclair (New York: Oxford University Press, 1961), pt. I, line 30.

14. In his *Archetypes and the Collective Unconscious*, Jung defines an archetype as "not personal" (4); an "archaic, primordial type" that is "universal" (5); a structure that occurs in myth, is found in every individual, and is expressive of the fantasy element of reality (67). These definitions are Jung's attempts to distinguish his collective psychology from Freud's personal psychology.

3—The Old Man and Echo

1. Ovid, "The Story of Echo and Narcissus," in *Metamorphoses*, trans. Rolfe Humphries (Bloomington, Ind.: Indiana University Press, 1958), 67–73.

2. See Patricia Berry, "Echo and Beauty," *Spring* (1980):59.

3. Jean-Jacques Mayoux, *Samuel Beckett* (Harlow, Essex: Longman Group, 1954), 5.

4. Harvey, *Samuel Beckett*, 69.

5. Uselessness, frustration, melancholy, depression—such states of physical slowness and torpor are essential to psychological reawakening. This is basic premise of James Hillman, who, in *Re-Visioning Psychology* (New York: Harper & Row, 1975), provides an analogy between the symbol system of alchemy, with its bizarre and pathological images, and the reawakening processes of soul. Hillman says, "The alchemist projected his depths into his materials, and while working upon them he was working also upon his soul. . . . The fire he tended and regulated with careful exactitude was the intensity of his own spirit, his failing or burning interest" (90).

6. For this insight into the relation of hands and the relative importance of left over right handling on Molloy's stick, I am indebted to my student, Julie Schofield, at the University of Redlands.

7. Murray Stein, "Narcissus," *Spring* (1976):52.

8. Gaston Bachelard, *L'eau et les rêves* (Paris: J. Corti, 1942), 33. Bachelard's remarks on the "open way" relate strikingly with Beckett's remarks, who also draws attention to the "open way" of art: "une petite overture, c'est un long chemin ouvert, vers le neant," (a little opening is a wide open way, toward nothing) in *Bram Van Velde: Les lithographies* (Geneve: Yves Riviere, 1974), 15–16. Accordingly, the "open way" connects Beckett not only with ancient myth but also with modern painting.

9. See Beryle S. Fletcher and John Fletcher, *A Student's Guide to the Plays of Samuel Beckett* (London: Faber and Faber, 1985). Besides the image of "head as cavern," Beckett has also used the image of "head with windows." Molloy says, "In my head there are several windows, that I do know, but perhaps it is always the same one, open variously on the parading universe. . . . And these different windows that open in my head, when I grope again among those days, really existed perhaps" (M, 51). In *Endgame*, blind Hamm is enclosed within the sealed jar (as Molloy would put it [M, 49]) of a room with two windows (eyes) to the outer world. Clov, Hamm's helper, is the interpreter of this outer world. But because Clov is associated with the cloven-footed one (the devil), there is the suggestion that Hamm's relation to outer experience will be through the eyes of the devil, who will lead Hamm down, not out.

10. Gaston Bachelard, *The Poetics of Reverie*, trans. Daniel Russell (Boston: Beacon Press, 1971), 111. A downward pull of the psyche, Bachelard says, draws the soul's eye to littler matters and to a deviant, not mind's eye way of seeing.

11. C. G. Jung, "Ulysses," CW 15, 119.

12. Berry, "Echo," 51.

13. James Joyce, *A Portrait of the Artist as a Young Man* (New York: Penguin Books, 1987), 213.

14. For an excellent discussion of the psychological significance of "coagulation," drawing on traditions of alchemy, neo-Platonism, and neo-Jungianism, see David L. Miller, *Three Faces of God: Traces of the Trinity in Literature and Life* (Philadelphia: Fortress Press, 1986), 88–91.

15. Winnie, in Beckett's *Happy Days*, recounts the words of Shower—or Cooker—who seeks the "idea," not the image, of Winnie stuck in the sand. "What does it mean? he says—What's it meant to mean?" (43). But the "meaning" of Winnie's image is not ideational; it is elemental: forged from the fires (Cookers) or waters (Showers) of the image itself.

4—Storytelling: The Stone of Cronus

1. Portions of this chapter appear as "Rites of Story: The Old Man at Play," in *Myth and Ritual in the Plays of Samuel Beckett*, ed. Katherine H. Burkman (Cranbury, N.J.: Fairleigh Dickinson University Press, 1987): 73–85.

2. See, for instance, Judith E. Dearlove, "The Voice and Its Words: 'How It Is in Beckett's Canon,' " *Journal of Beckett Studies* 3 (Summer 1978):56–75; Ted Estess, "The 'Inenarrable Contraption': Reflections on the Metaphor of Story," *Journal of the American Academy of Religion* 42, no. 3 (September 1974):415–34; Bruce Kawin, *Telling It Again and Again: Repetition in Literature and Film* (Ithaca, N.Y.: Cornell University Press, 1972); and James Hansford, "Seeing and Saying in *As the Story was Told*," *Journal of Beckett Studies* 8 (Autumn 1982):75–94.

3. Gontarski, "The World Première," 135.

4. Mircea Eliade, *The Sacred and the Profane: The Nature of Religion*, trans. Willard R. Trask (New York: Harcourt Brace, 1968), 70.

5. Jung, "Archetypes of the Collective Unconscious" in CW 9, 1 *Archetypes and the Collective Unconscious*, 26–27.

6. The head "as seat of consciousness," where imaginary leaps can take place, is discussed by Jung in his work with hermetic symbols in his CW 13 *Alchemical Studies* (1968), 72, 80, 240.

7. Katharine J. Worth, "Beckett's Fine Shades," *Journal of Beckett Studies* no. 1 (Winter 1976):76.

8. Quoted in A. Vitale, "Saturn: The Transformation of the Father," in *Fathers and Mothers: Essays by Five Hands* (New York/Zurich: Spring Publications, 1974), 27.

9. "One begins at last to see, in the night. In the night which is dawn and noon and evening and night in a wide sky, in a still land," translation mine (Beckett, *Peintres*, 3). Night seeing, thus, renders darkness its own natural setting, totally unrelated with either negatives or pessimisms.

10. For more on the significance of the "left" side of Beckett's characters, particularly his women, see chapter 5, pp. 64–65.

11. Zazen refers to the cross-legged sitting position used during Zen Buddhist meditation.

12. Ferdinand de Saussure, "Langue et parole," *Cours de la linguistique générale* (Paris: Payot, 1961).

13. George Steiner, *Language and Silence: Essays on Language, Literature and Film* (New York: Atheneum Press, 1967), 42.

14. Philip Wheelwright, *Metaphor and Reality* (Bloomington, Ind.: Indiana University Press, 1968), 134–35.

15. The word "fancy" is not associated with the old man but rather with the female characters—most notably in *Footfalls*. The old man, however, uses his head as a place for fancy, a fantasy place, where reality acquires night seeing.

5—Measures of Despair: The Demeter Myth

1. This chapter was written originally with the help of a grant from the State University of New York Summer Research Foundation (1982), and is published in *The Journal of Beckett Studies*, no. 11 (Spring 1988); it also contains segments from "Walking and Rocking: Ritual Acts in *Footfalls* and *Rockaby*," in *Make Sense Who May* (edited by Robin J. Davis and Lance St. John Butler: New York: Barnes and Noble, 1988). The chapter presented here has been extensively revised.

2. See Lawrence Graver and Raymond Federman, eds., *Samuel Beckett: The Critical Heritage* (London: Routledge & Kegan Paul, 1979):328–29, 333, 342.

3. For more on the *via negativa*, or negative way, as a cultural pattern see Mircea Eliade, *The Forge and the Crucible: The Origins and Structures of Alchemy*, trans. Stephen Corrin (New York: Harper & Row, 1971):149–51; James Hillman, *Re-Visioning Psychology* (New York: Harper & Row, 1975), 197; and Matthew Fox, *Original Blessing: A Primer in Creation Spirituality* (Santa Fe, N.M.: Bear and Company, 1986), 146–47.

4. Moore, *Rituals*, 21.

5. Beckett's titles are richly suggestive, as these few samples indicate. See *The Lost Ones* (New York, Grove Press, 1972), *All Strange Away* (New York: Gotham Book Mart Master Series, 1976; *Come and Go* (London: Calder and Boyars, 1967), and *Ghost Trio*, in *Ends and Odds* (New York: Grove Press, 1976). For a psychological interpretation of threeness, as in *Ghost Trio*, see Miller, *Three Faces of God*.

6. For drawing my attention to Beckett's early work and to specific lines in Beckett's poetry, I am indebted to Rubin Rabinovitz. The poem appears in *Samuel Beckett, Collected Poems in French and English* (New York: Grove Press, 1977), 51.

7. This poem is one of the few not translated by Beckett from the original French into English. For whatever reason Beckett chose not to translate this poem, I wish the original to stand, with explication arising from textual discussion. Like Vivian Mercier, in his *Beckett/Beckett* (243), I have "misgivings" about attempting what Beckett, who translated his own works into French and German, did not (in this case) do.

8. The phrase "exquisite feminine greyness" is Ruby Cohn's and refers originally to Winnie's predicament. See Cohn's *Just Play: Beckett's Theater* (Princeton: Princeton University Press, 1980), 270.

9. See my review of this Los Angeles production of *Happy Days* in "The Beckett Circle," eds. Lois More Overbeck and Martha Fehsenfeld, 9 no. 2 (Spring 1987), 3.

10. Winnie's mouse, like Jung's rat, functions to disturb boredom out of its normalcy. The rat of latent unconscious contents does the same thing by gnawing at the psyche. For comment on the rat as psychic image see Jung, "The Functions of the Unconscious," in CW 18 *Symbolic Life,* 196.

11. "The Homeric Hymn to Demeter," in *The Homeric Hymns and Homerica,* trans. G. Evelyn-White (Cambridge, Mass.: Harvard University Press, 1964), 288–323. Further references to this work, cited by line, will be incorporated into the text.

12. These are the final lines in Beckett's *Ill Seen Ill Said,* 59, translated from the French by Beckett. I take exception to the generally accepted view that Beckett's pun on "know" is ironic, since I place Beckett's negativism not in philosophy but in myth. For a reading of irony in these lines see Monique Nagem's "Know Happiness: Irony in *Ill Seen Ill Said,*" in a collection that also features my article, "Walking and Rocking: Ritual Acts in *Footfalls* and *Rockaby,*" in *Make Sense Who May.*

13. The quotations were those of Beckett as stated by Dina Sherzer, "Towards an Aesthetic of the Un-word," a paper delivered at a symposium entitled "Samuel Beckett: Humanistic Perspectives" (Columbus, Ohio, May 1981).

14. Billie Whitelaw's responses to playing this part have already been noted in chapter 1. An experienced actress, she conveys to us some of the physical difficulty in being confined and confused—as Mouth must be. For younger actresses the part has perhaps a more devastating effect. Alex Sommer, who played Mouth for the Beckett Conference at Stirling, Scotland (August 1986), was visibly unnerved when I saw her after her performance. For the rest of the evening, her hands could not stop shaking and she could hardly focus her speech.

15. See Eliade, *Sacred;* and for Eliade's three stages of ritual action, see his *Cosmos and History: The Myth of the Eternal Return,* trans. Willard R. Trask (New York: Harper and Brothers, 1959), 14, 12, 18.

16. Murray Stein, *In Midlife: A Jungian Perspective* (Dallas, Tex.: Spring Publications, 1983), 126. Other references to this work are cited by page number in the text.

17. See *Plato's Phaedrus,* trans. R. Hackforth (New York: Cambridge University Press, 1972), where souls, racked with two steeds, confounded and confused, "baulked, every one, of the full vision of Being, and departing therefrom, they *feed upon the food of semblance*" (79), italics mine. In his rehearsal notes on *Footfalls,* with Beckett directing, Walter Asmus taped Beckett's comments to the actress playing May, Hildegard Schmahl: "You are looking for words which are as food for the poor girl, you correct yourself constantly" ("Practical Aspects of Theater, Radio and Television: Rehearsal Notes for the German Première of *That Time* and *Footfalls,*" *Journal of Beckett Studies* no. 2 [Summer 1977], 86). In that same article Asmus conveys some wonderfully telling comments by Beckett; namely, that May is in the play "exclusively for herself. She is isolated. The costume will look like a ghost costume. . . . It is the costume of a ghost" (85). This comment coincides with Beckett's earlier explanation to the actress that the girl May is like the girl in Jung's lecture (at the Tavistock clinic) who existed but was not actually living because she hadn't been born (83). Asmus writes, "There is the connection with the Jung story. A life, which didn't begin as a life, but which was just there, as a thing" (84). When Beckett called May's sequel a pun "Sequel = seek well," (Asmus, 85), we get further insight into a deeply mythopoetic basis of the play's mother-daughter relationship, where seeking well is also seeking by the well, and seeking from the wellspring.

18. Katherine H. Burkman, "Initiation Rites in Samuel Beckett's *Waiting for Godot,*" *Papers in Comparative Studies* 3 (1984), 141.

19. Being "right-minded" or "right-handed" suggests that a person is orthodox by following a straight path which, because it does not deviate, is not devious. To be left-handed, or in this case, left-footed, suggests that there is a basic deviation at work, a sinister straying from the norm. But as I suggested in chapter two note 13 (by a reference to Dante), the left-footed quester is the one most likely to achieve transformation.

20. Robert Sardello, "The Landscape of Virginity," in *Images of the Untouched,* eds. Joanne Stroud and Gail Thomas (Dallas, Tex.: Spring Publications, 1982), 44.

21. Patricia Berry, "The Rape of Demeter/Persephone and Neurosis," *Spring* (1975), 197–98.

22. Interestingly, whereas nine steps is a really insistent part of the German production (see Asmus, p. 84), it was not a part of the original Royal Court production in London, as first printings of *Footfalls* will attest. When I asked Walter Asmus about this (Stirling, Scotland at the International Beckett Conference, August 1986), he expressed amusement, surprise, even disbelief, and could supply no reason for the switch in number, except that the stage at the Royal Court may have been longer, requiring one additional footstep.

23. Suzanne Langer, *Feeling and Form* (New York: Scribner's, 1953), 50.

24. This chapter has been more concerned with the movement of a come-and-go pattern for animation of soul—a pattern true of Beckett's women. But even Beckett's male characters have a kind of animation in their refusal to move. Consider the ending of *The Unnamable*: "in the silence you don't know, you must go on, I can't go on, I'll go on" (414); consider Gogo's commitment to Didi, in *Waiting for Godot*, where remaining is a stronger possibility for action than going. This kind of negative action or active inaction is a phenomenon noted by Patricia Berry, in "Stopping as a Mode of Animation," paper delivered at a symposium entitled "Anima, Animals, Animation" (Buffalo, N.Y.: November 1980).

25. See *The American Heritage Dictionary of the English Language,* ed. William Morris (N.Y.: Houghton Mifflin Co., 1969). The accompanying illustration of the defined word "rack" (p. 1075 of this *Dictionary*) gives the image of forward-and-circular movement in a line-and-circle pattern that describes other contradictory movements in Beckett's work.

26. In pronouncing the words "but the clouds" in Beckett's play by the same name, Billie Whitelaw dropped her jaw at each vowel sound while the camera did a closeup on her face with its unblinking eyes. The effect was haunting, almost as if it were an image in mood and sight of May's strange phrase "like moon through passing . . . rack."

6—The Myth of the Eternal Regression

1. See Eliade, *Cosmos and History,* 84. See also Eliade, *The Quest: History and Meaning in Religion* (Chicago: University of Chicago Press, 1975), 82.

2. James Hillman, "Anima Mundi and the Imagination of Postmodern Therapy." (Paper delivered at a conference sponsored by the Center for a Postmodern World, Santa Barbara, Calif., January 1987).

3. James Hillman, *Archetypal Psychology: A Brief Account* (Dallas, Tex.: Spring Publications, 1985), 22–23.

4. Marjorie Perloff, "Beckett and the New Poetry." (Paper delivered at the Beckett Session of the annual conference of the Modern Language Association, N.Y.C., 28 December 1981).

5. Edward Gorey's drawings, in a series of sixteen small boxes, give a similar prehistoric sense in his illustrations of Beckett's *All Strange Away* (New York: Gotham Book Mart, 1976). Nettles, rocks, caves; beehive tombs; crooked, peeling walls; boney, meatless spikes—drawn in barely recognizable shapes and contrasting textures of black and white—provide Beckett's phrase "flowing and ebbing" with a feeling of being in an "under" kingdom.

6. Beckett's interest in patterns, repeated but on different levels, is consistent with an imagination that blends mathematical precision with flowing shapes. It also explains why Beckett's work lends itself to so many different artistic disciplines—everything from radio and television, to

stage and screen, to dance and music hall. *Footfalls*, for instance, was adapted by the Compagnie Maguy Marin to a dance theater piece called, punningly, "May B."

7. See Miller, "The Critic as Host," in *Deconstruction*, 252.

8. See Jacques Derrida, "Living On," trans. James Hulbert, in *Deconstruction*, 130.

9. What for Martin Buber is an I-Thou relationship is for Carl Jung an I-You relationship, as in Jung's statement, "the soul cannot exist without its other side, which is always found in a 'You,' " in *The Practice of Psychotherapy*, CW 16, 454. Beckett's is an I-It relationship.

10. Jung, "The Child Archetype," in CW 9, 1 *Archetypes*, 161, footnote. For a concise definition of "archetype," see J. E. Dearlove, "Allusion to Archetype," *Journal of Beckett Studies* no. 10 (1985):126.

11. Yasunari Takahashi, "Samuel Beckett and the Noh," *Encounter* (April 1982):58, 73. At the symposium entitled "Samuel Beckett: Humanistic Perspectives" in Columbus, Ohio (May 1981) an entire session was devoted to Beckett and Noh. Carol Sorgenfrei and Royall Tyler were the participants.

12. Merleau-Ponty, *The Visible*, 102.

13. See Jung, "The Language of Dreams," in CW 18 *Symbolic Life*, 209.

14. Lois More Overbeck, "What the Words Cannot Tell: Dramatic Image in Plays of Samuel Beckett." (Paper delivered at the Twentieth-Century Literature conference, Louisville, KY, February 1985).

15. Richard Ellman, "Samuel Beckett: Nayman of Noland," Washington, D.C.: Library of Congress, 1986, last page.

16. Chabert, "Dire Beckett." (Paper delivered at a conference entitled "Beckett Dans Le Siècle," Paris, France, 26 April 1986).

Bibliography

I. Samuel Beckett—Primary Sources

All Strange Away. New York: Gotham Book Mart, 1976.

All That Fall. New York: Grove Press, 1957.

Bram van Velde. New York: Grove Press, 1960.

Bram van Velde: les lithographies. Geneve: Yves Riviere, 1974.

Cascando and Other Short Dramatic Pieces. New York: Grove Press, 1969.

Collected Poems in French and English. New York: Grove Press, 1977.

Come and Go. In *Cascando and Other Short Dramatic Pieces.* New York: Grove Press, 1969.

Company. New York: Grove Press, 1980.

"Dante . . . Bruno. Vico . . Joyce." *Our Exagmination Round his Factification for Incamination of Work in Progress.* Paris: Shakespeare and Company, 1929, 1–22. Reprint Northampton, England: John Dickens and Conner, 1962.

"Denis Devlin." Review of "Intercessions," by Denis Devlin. *transition: Tenth Anniversary* 27 (April–May 1938):289–94.

"Les deux besoins." In "Samuel Beckett on Life, Art and Criticism," by Lawrence E. Harvey. *Modern Language Notes* 80 (December 1965):548ff.

"Echo's Bones." In *Collected Poems in French and English.* New York: Grove Press, 1961.

Embers. In *Krapp's Last Tape and Other Dramatic Pieces.* New York: Grove Press, 1960.

"The End." In *Stories and Texts for Nothing.* New York: Grove Press, 1967.

Endgame: A Play in One Act. New York: Grove Press, 1958.

Ends and Odds: Eight New Dramatic Pieces. New York: Grove Press, 1976.

"The Essential and the Incidental." Review of *Windfalls* by Sean O'Casey. *The Bookman* 87 (Christmas 1934):111.

"Ex Cathezra." Review of *Make It New,* by Ezra Pound. *The Bookman* 87 (Christmas 1934):10.

The most complete bibliography of Samuel Beckett is to be found in Raymond Federman and John Fletcher, *Samuel Beckett: His Works and His Critics, An Essay in Bibliography* (Berkeley: University of California Press, 1970). Since its publication, a year after Beckett won the Nobel Prize for literature, scholarly works on Beckett have proliferated to the extent that the Bibliography is now virtually out of date. The following list includes the major works consulted and reflects the interdisciplinary nature of this study.

Footfalls. In *Ends and Odds: Eight New Dramatic Pieces.* New York: Grove Press, 1976.

Happy Days. New York: Grove Press, 1961.

"Henri Hayden, homme-peintre." *Henri Hayden Recent Paintings* (catalogue). London: Waddington Galleries, February 1959, 2.

"Hommage à Jack B. Yeats." In *Les Lettres Nouvelles* 2 (April 1954):619–20.

How It Is. New York: Grove Press, 1964.

"Humanistic Quietism." Review of *Poems,* by Thomas McGreevy. *Dublin Magazine* 9 (July–September 1934):79–80.

Ill Seen Ill Said. New York: Grove Press, 1981.

"An Imaginative Work!" Review of *The Amaranthers,* by Jack B. Yeats. *Dublin Magazine* 11, no. 3 (July–September 1936):80–81.

Krapp's Last Tape and Other Dramatic Pieces (includes *Embers* and *All That Fall*). New York: Grove Press, 1960.

The Lost Ones. New York: Grove Press, 1972.

"McGreevy on Yeats." Review of *Jack B. Yeats,* by Thomas McGreevy. *Irish Times* (4 August 1945):2.

Molloy in *Three Novels by Samuel Beckett.* New York: Grove Press, 1965.

Murphy. New York: Grove Press, 1957.

Not I. In *Ends and Odds: Eight New Dramatic Pieces.* New York: Grove Press, 1976.

Ohio Impromptu. In *Rockaby and Other Short Pieces.* New York: Grove Press, 1981.

"Papini's Dante." Review of Dante by Giovanni Papini. *The Bookman* 87 (Christmas 1934):14.

"Peintres de l'empêchement." *Derrière le miroir,* nos. 11 and 12 (June 1948):3–7.

"La Peinture des van Velde, ou: le monde et le pantalon." *Les cahiers d'art* (1945–46), 349–56.

"Poetry Is Vertical." Manifesto. In *transition* 21 (March 1932):148–49.

Proust. New York: Grove Press, 1931.

Quad. London: Faber and Faber, 1984.

"Recent Irish Poetry." *The Bookman* 77 (August 1934):241–42.

Rockaby and Other Short Pieces. New York: Grove Press, 1981.

Stories and Texts for Nothing. New York: Grove Press, 1967.

That Time. In *Ends and Odds: Eight New Dramatic Pieces.* New York: Grove Press, 1976.

"Three Dialogues." *transition Forty-Nine* 5 (December 1949):97–103.

Three Novels: Molloy, Malone Dies, The Unnamable. Trans. Patrick Bowles and Samuel Beckett. New York: Grove Press, 1965.

The Unnamable. In *Three Novels by Samuel Beckett.* New York: Grove Press, 1965.

Waiting for Godot. New York: Grove Press, 1954.

Watt. New York: Grove Press, 1970.

What Where. In *Ohio Impromptu, Catastrophe, and What Where: Three Plays by Samuel Beckett.* New York: Grove Press, 1984.

Words and Music. London: Faber and Faber, 1964.

II. Samuel Beckett—Secondary Sources

Abbott, H. Porter. *The Fiction of Samuel Beckett: Form and Effect.* Berkeley, Calif.: University of California Press, 1973.

Asmus, Walter. "Practical Aspects of Theater, Radio and Television: Rehearsal Notes for the German Première of *That Time* and *Footfalls.*" Trans. Helen Watanabe. *Journal of Beckett Studies,* no. 2 (Summer 1977):82–95.

Bair, Deirdre. *Samuel Beckett: A Biography.* New York: Harcourt Brace Jovanovich, 1978.

Barnard, G. C. *Samuel Beckett: A New Approach.* New York: Dodd, 1970.

Beckett at 60: A Festschrift. London: Calder and Boyars, 1967.

Blau, Herbert. *The Eye of the Prey: Subversions of the Postmodern.* Bloomington, Ind.: Indiana University Press, 1987.

———. *The Impossible Theater: A Manifesto.* New York: Macmillan, 1961.

Brienza, Susan D. "Perilous Journeys on Beckett's Stages: Travelling Through Words." In *Myth and Ritual in the Plays of Samuel Beckett.* Cranbury, N.J.: Fairleigh Dickinson Press, 1987:28–49.

———. *Samuel Beckett's New Worlds: Styles of Metafiction.* Norman, Okla.: University of Oklahoma Press, 1987.

Burkman, Katherine H. "Initiation Rites in Samuel Beckett's *Waiting for Godot.*" *Papers in Comparative Studies* 3 (1984):137–52.

———. ed. *Myth and Ritual in the Plays of Samuel Beckett.* Cranbury, N.J.: Fairleigh Dickinson Press, 1987.

Chabert, Pierre. "Dire Beckett." Paper presented at a conference entitled Beckett Dans Le Siècle, Paris, France, April 1986.

Christensen, Inger. *The Meaning of Metafiction: A Critical Study of Selected Novels by Sterne, Nabokov, Barth and Beckett.* New York: Columbia University Press, 1981.

Coe, Richard N. *Samuel Beckett.* New York: Grove Press, 1964.

Cohn, Ruby. *Back to Beckett.* Princeton, N.J.: Princeton University Press, 1973.

———. *Just Play: Beckett's Theater.* Princeton, N.J.: Princeton University Press, 1980.

———. *Samuel Beckett: The Comic Gamut.* New Brunswick, N.J.: Rutgers University Press, 1962.

Copeland, Hannah Case. *Art and the Artist in the Works of Samuel Beckett.* The Hague: Mouton and Co., 1975.

Cordero, Anne D. "Waiting, An Ambivalent Mood in Beckett and Ionesco." *Studies in the Twentieth Century* (ed. Stephen H. Goode), 13 (Spring 1974):51–63.

Davis, Robin J., and Lance St. John Butler, eds. *Make Sense Who May.* New York: Barnes and Noble, 1988.

Dearlove, J. E. "Allusion to Archetype," *Journal of Beckett Studies,* no. 10 (1985):121–33.

———. "The Voice and Its Words." *Journal of Beckett Studies* 3 (Summer 1978):56–75.

Driver, Tom F. "Beckett by the Madeleine." *Columbia University Forum* 4 (Summer 1961):21–25.

Duckworth, Colin. *Angels of Darkness.* New York: Barnes and Noble Books, 1972.

Eliopolos, James. *Samuel Beckett's Dramatic Language.* Hawthorne, N.Y.: Mouton Publishing Co., 1975.

Ellman, Richard. "Samuel Beckett: Nayman of Noland." Paper. Washington, D.C.: Library of Congress, 1986.

Esslin, Martin. "Samuel Beckett: The Search for Self." In *The Theater of the Absurd*, ed. Esslin, 1–46. New York: Doubleday, Anchor Books, 1961.

———. ed. *Samuel Beckett: A Collection of Critical Essays*. Englewood Cliffs, N.J.: Prentice-Hall, 1965.

Estess, Ted L. "The 'Inenarrable Contraption': Reflections of the Metaphor of Story." *Journal of the American Academy of Religion* 42, no. 3 (September 1974):415–34.

Federman, Raymond. *Journey to Chaos: Samuel Beckett's Early Fiction*. Berkeley, Calif.: University of California Press, 1965.

Federman, Raymond, and John Fletcher. *Samuel Beckett: His Works and His Critics, An Essay in Bibliography*. Berkeley, Calif.: University of California Press, 1970.

Fletcher, Beryle S., and John Fletcher. *A Student's Guide to the Plays of Samuel Beckett*. London: Faber and Faber, 1985.

Fletcher, John. *The Novels of Samuel Beckett*. London: Chatto and Windus, 1964.

———. *Samuel Beckett's Art*. London: Chatto and Windus, 1967.

Fletcher, John, and John Spurling. *Beckett: A Study of His Plays*. New York: Hill and Wang, 1972.

Friedman, Melvin J., ed. *Samuel Beckett Now: Critical Approaches to His Novels, Poetry and Plays*. Chicago: University of Chicago Press, 1970.

Gerard, Martin. "Molloy Becomes Unnamable." *X, A Quarterly Review* 1, no. 4 (October 1960):314–19.

Gontarski, S. E. *The Intent of Undoing in Samuel Becektt's Dramatic Texts*. Bloomington, Ind.: Indiana University Press, 1985.

———. "The World Première of *Ohio Impromptu*." *Journal of Beckett Studies*, no. 8 (Autumn 1982):133–35.

Graver, Lawrence, and Raymond Federman, eds. *Samuel Beckett: The Critical Heritage*. London: Routledge & Kegan Paul, 1979.

Hamilton, Carol. "Portrait of Old Age: The Image of Man in Beckett's Trilogy." *Western Humanities Review* 16 (Spring 1962):157–65.

Hansford, James. "Seeing and Saying in 'As the Story was Told.' " *Journal of Beckett Studies* 8 (Autumn 1982):75–94.

Harvey, Lawrence E. *Samuel Beckett: Poet and Critic*. Princeton: Princeton University Press, 1970.

Hassan, Ihab. *The Literature of Silence: Henry Miller and Samuel Beckett*. New York: Alfred A. Knopf, 1967.

Hesla, David H. *The Shape of Chaos: An Interpretation of the Art of Samuel Beckett*. Minneapolis, Minn.: University of Minnesota Press, 1971.

Hubert, Renée Riese. "The Couple and the Performance in Samuel Beckett's Plays." *Esprit Créateur* 2 (Winter 1962):175–80.

Jacobsen, Josephine, and William R. Mueller. "Samuel Beckett's Long Saturday: To Wait or Not to Wait?" In *Man in the Modern Theater*, ed. Martin Esslin (Richmond, Va.: John Knox Press, 1965), 76–97.

Kawin, Bruce F. *Telling it Again and Again: Repetition in Literature and Film*. Ithaca, N.Y.: Cornell University Press, 1972.

Kelly, Katherine. "The Orphic Mouth in *Not I*." *Journal of Beckett Studies*, no. 6 (Autumn 1980):73–80.

Kennedy, Sighle. *Murphy's Bed: A Study of Real Sources and Sur-real Associations in Samuel Beckett's First Novel*. Lewisburg, Pa.: Bucknell University Press, 1971.

Kenner, Hugh. *Samuel Beckett: A Critical Study*. New York: Grove Press, 1961.

Kern, Edith. "Moran-Molloy: The Hero as Author." *Perspective* 11, no. 3 (Autumn 1959):183–93.

Knowlson, James. "*Krapp's Last Tape:* The Evolution of a Play, 1958–75." *Journal of Beckett Studies*, no. 1 (Winter 1976):50–65.

Knowlson, James and John Pilling. *Frescoes of the Skull: The Later Prose and Drama of Samuel Beckett*. London: Calder, 1979.

Mayoux, Jean-Jacques. *Samuel Beckett*. Harlow, Essex: Longman Group, 1974.

Mercier, Vivian. *Beckett/Beckett*. New York: Oxford University Press, 1977.

Metman, Eva. "Reflections on Samuel Beckett's Plays." In *Samuel Beckett: A Collection of Critical Essays*, ed. Martin Esslin, 117–39. Englewood Cliffs, N.J.: Prentice-Hall, 1965.

Mintz, Samuel I. "Beckett's *Murphy*: A 'Cartesian' Novel." *Perspective* 11 (Autumn 1959):156–65.

Mooney, Michael E. "Beckett's 'Discourse on Method.' " *Journal of Beckett Studies* 3 (Summer 1978):40–55.

O'Hara, J. D. "Jung and the Narratives of *Molloy*." *Journal of Beckett Studies* no. 7 (Spring 1982):19–48.

Overbeck, Lois More. "What the Words Cannot Tell: Dramatic Image in Plays of Samuel Beckett." Paper presented to the Twentieth Century Literature Conference, Louisville, Kentucky, February 1985.

Perloff, Marjorie. "Beckett and the New Poetry." Paper delivered at the Beckett Session of Modern Language Association Conference. New York, N.Y.: 28 December 1981.

Pilling, John. "Beckett's *Proust*." *Journal of Beckett Studies*, no. 1 (Winter 1976):8–29.

Pountney, Rosemary. "On Acting Mouth in *Not I*." *Journal of Beckett Studies*, no. 1 (Winter 1976):81–85.

Rabinovitz, Rubin. "*Molloy* and the Archetypal Traveller." *Journal of Beckett Studies*, no. 5 (Autumn 1979):25–44.

————. "Repetition and Underlying Meanings in Samuel Beckett's Trilogy." Keynote address delivered to the International Beckett conference at the University of Stirling, Scotland. August 1986.

Rickels, Milton. "Existential Themes in Beckett's *Unnamable*." *Criticism* 4 (Spring 1962):134–47.

Robinson, Michael. *The Long Sonata of the Dead: A Study of Samuel Beckett*. New York: Grove Press, 1970.

Romano, John. "Beckett Without Angst." *American Scholar* 47 (Winter 1977):96–102.

Rosen, Steven J. *Samuel Beckett and the Pessimistic Tradition*. New Brunswick, N.J.: Rutgers University Press, 1976.

Scholes, Robert. "The Fictional Criticism of the Future." *Triquarterly* 34 (Fall 1975):233–47.

Scott, Nathan A., Jr. *Samuel Beckett.* Hewlett, N.Y.: Hilary House, 1965.
Shenker, Israel. "Moody Man of Letters" (interview). *New York Times,* 6 May 1956, sec. 2 p. 1, 3.
Sherzer, Dina. "Towards an Aesthetic of the Un-word." Paper delivered at a symposium entitled "Samuel Beckett: Humanistic Perspectives." Ohio State University, Columbus, Ohio, May 1981.
Szanto, George H. *Narrative Consciousness: Structure and Perception in the Fiction of Kafka, Beckett and Robbe-Grillet.* Austin, Tex.: University of Texas Press, 1972.
Takahashi, Yasunari. "Samuel Beckett and the Noh." *Encounter* 58 (April 1982):56–73.
Worth, Katharine J., ed. *Beckett the Shape Changer: A Symposium.* London: Routledge & Kegan Paul, 1975.
———. "Beckett's Fine Shades." *Journal of Beckett Studies,* no. 1 (Winter 1976):75–80.

III. Archetypal Psychology

Bachelard, Gaston. *L'eau et les rêves: Essai sur l'imagination de la matière.* Paris: J. Corti, 1942.
———. *The Poetics of Reverie: Childhood, Language and the Cosmos.* Trans. Daniel Russell. Boston, Mass.: Beacon Press, 1971.
———. *The Poetics of Space.* Trans. Maria Jolas. Boston, Mass.: Beacon Press, 1964.
———. *The Psychoanalysis of Fire.* Trans. Alan C. M. Ross. Boston, Mass.: Beacon Press, 1968.
Baird, James. "Jungian Psychology in Criticism." *Yearbook of Comparative Criticism* 7 (August 1976):3–30.
Berry, Patricia. "An Approach to the Dream." *Spring: An Annual of Archetypal Psychology and Jungian Thought* (1976):58–79. Hereafter cited as *Spring.*
———. "Echo and Beauty." *Spring* (1980):49–59.
———. "The Rape of Demeter/Persephone and Neurosis." *Spring* (1975):186–98.
Boer, Charles. "Poetry and Psyche." *Spring* (1979):93–101.
Campbell, Joseph. *The Hero With a Thousand Faces.* Cleveland, Ohio: World Publishing Co., 1949.
Casey, Edward S. "Toward an Archetypal Imagination." *Spring* (1974):1–32.
———. "Toward a Phenomenology of the Imagination." *Journal of the British Society for Phenomenology* 5, no. 1 (January 1974):3–19.
Claremont de Castillejo, Irene. *Knowing Woman: A Feminine Psychology.* New York: Harper & Row, 1973.
Edinger, Edward. *Ego and Archetype: Individuation and the Religious Function of the Psyche.* New York: G. P. Putnam's Sons, 1972.
Entralgo, Pedro Lain. *The Therapy of the Word in Classical Antiquity.* Trans. L. J. Rather and J. M. Sharp. New Haven, Conn.: Yale University Press, 1970.
Hillman, James. "Abandoning the Child." In his *Loose Ends: Primary Papers in Archetypal Psychology.* Zurich: Spring Publications, 1975, 5–48. Hereafter cited as *Loose Ends.*

―――. "Anima Mundi and the Imagination of Postmodern Therapy." Paper delivered at a conference sponsored by the Center for a Postmodern World. Santa Barbara, Calif.: January 1987.

―――. *Archetypal Psychology: A Brief Account*. Dallas, Tex.: Spring Publications, 1985.

―――. "Betrayal." *Loose Ends*, 63–81.

―――. *The Dream and the Underworld*. New York: Harper & Row, 1979.

―――. "The Fiction of Case History: A Round." *Religion and Story*, ed. James Wiggins. New York: Harper & Row, 1975, 123–74.

―――. "Going Bugs." Paper delivered at a conference entitled "Anima, Animals, Animation." Buffalo, New York: November 1980.

―――. "An Inquiry into Image." *Spring* (1977):62–88.

―――. "The 'Negative' Senex and a Renaissance Solution." *Spring* (1975):77–109.

―――. "A Note on Story." *Parabola: Myth and the Quest for Meaning* 4, no. 4 (November 1979):43–45.

―――. "On Psychological Language." In his *Myth of Analysis: Three Essays in Archetypal Psychology*. Evanston, Ill.: Northwestern University Press, 1972, 117–214.

―――. "On Psychological Creativity." In his *Myth of Analysis*, 11–116.

―――. "On Senex Consciousness." *Spring* (1970):146–65.

―――. "Peaks and Vales." In *Puer Papers*. Irving, Tex.: Spring Publications, 1979, 54–76.

―――. "Pothos: The Nostalgis of the Puer Eternus." In his *Loose Ends*, 49–62.

―――. *Re-Visioning Psychology*. New York: Harper & Row, 1975.

―――. "Schism as Differing Visions." In his *Loose Ends*, 82–97.

―――. "Senex and Puer." In *Puer Papers*, 3–53.

Jung, C. G. *The Collected Works* (Cited as CW in text). Trans. R. F. C. Hull. Eds. Sir Herbert Read, Michael Fordham, Gerhard Adler, William McGuire. Princeton, N.J.: Princeton University Press, Bollingen Series 20, 1952–1978.

―――. *Aion: Researches into the Phenomenology of the Self*. Vol. 9, pt. 2 (1968).

―――. *The Archetypes and the Collective Unconscious*. Vol. 9, pt. 1 (1968).

―――. *Modern Man in Search of a Soul*. Trans. W. S. Dell and Cary F. Barnes. New York: Harcourt, Brace & Co., 1933.

―――. *The Practice of Psychotherapy*. Vol. 16 (1966).

―――. *Psychology and Alchemy*. Vol. 12 (1968).

―――. *Psychology and Religion: East and West*. Vol. 11 (1969).

―――. *The Spirit in Man, Art, and Literature*. Vol. 15 (1966).

―――. *The Symbolic Life*. Vol. 18 (1976).

―――. *Symbols of Transformation*. Vol. 5 (1967).

―――. *Two Essays on Analytical Psychology*. Vol. 7 (1966).

―――. *The Undiscovered Self*. Trans. R. F. C. Hull. Boston: Atlantic-Little, Brown Books, 1958.

Kerényi, Karl. "Man and Mask." *Spiritual Disciplines: Papers from the Eranos Yearbooks*. Trans. Ralph Manheim. New York: Pantheon Books, Bollingen Series 30. 1960, 151–67.

Kerényi, Karl, and C. G. Jung. *Essays on a Science of Mythology: The Myths of the Divine Child and the Divine Maiden.* Rev. ed. Trans. R. F. C. Hull. New York: Harper & Row, 1963, 70–100.

McGuire, William, ed. *The Freud/Jung Letters.* Princeton: Princeton University Press, 1974.

Meier, C. A. *Ancient Incubation and Modern Psychotherapy.* Evanston, Ill.: Northwestern University Press, 1968.

Micklem, Niel. "The Intolerable Image: The Mythic Background of Psychosis." *Spring* (1979):1–19.

Miller, David L. *Christs: Meditations on Archetypal Images in Christian Theology.* New York: The Seabury Press, 1981.

———. "Fairy Tale or Myth?" *Spring* (1976):157–64.

———. "The Gods and Soul: An Essay Review." *Journal of the American Academy of Religion* 43, no. 3 (September 1975):586–90.

———. "Hades and Dionysus: The Poetry of Soul." *Journal of the American Academy of Religion* 46, no. 3 (1978):331–335.

———. *Three Faces of God: Traces of the Trinity in Literature and Life.* Philadelphia: Fortress Press, 1986.

Moore, Tom. *Rituals of the Imagination.* Dallas, Tex.: The Pegasus Foundation, 1983.

Sardello, Robert. "The Landscape of Virginity." In *Images of the Untouched,* eds. Joanne Stroud and Gail Thomas. Dallas, Tex.: Spring Publications, 1982.

Stein, Murray. *In Midlife: A Jungian Perspective.* Dallas, Tex.: Spring Publications, 1983.

———. "Narcissus." *Spring* (1976):32–52.

Vitale, A. "Saturn: The Transformation of the Father." *Fathers and Mothers: Essays by Five Hands.* New York/Zurich: Spring Publications, 1974, 4–39.

Walker, Mitchell. "The Double: An Archetypal Configuration." *Spring* (1976):165–75.

Whitmont, Edward C. *The Symbolic Quest: Basic Concepts of Analytical Psychology.* New York: G. P. Putnam's, 1969.

IV. Hermeneutics of Religion, Myth, and Literature

Barfield, Owen. "The Meaning of the Word 'Literal.' " *Metaphor and Symbol,* ed. L. C. Knights and B. Cottle. London: Butterworths, 1960.

Bettelheim, Bruno. *The Uses of Enchantment: The Meaning and Importance of Fairy Tales.* New York: Alfred A. Knopf, 1976.

Brenneman, Walter L., Jr. *Spirals: A Study in Symbol, Myth and Ritual.* Lanham, Md.: University Press of America, 1978.

Brown, Norman. *Love's Body.* New York: Vintage Books, 1966.

Crites, Stephen. "The Narrative Quality of Experience." *Journal of American Academy of Religion* 39, no. 3 (September 1971):291–311.

Driver, Tom F. "The Sense of Words and the Sense of Action: A Gestalt Concerning Religion and Literature." LeMoyne College Forum on Religion and Literature, Syracuse, N.Y., 29 April 1979.

Eliade, Mircea. *Cosmos and History: The Myth of the Eternal Return.* Trans. Willard R. Trask. New York: Harper & Brothers, 1959.

———. *The Forge and the Crucible: The Origins and Structures of Alchemy.* Trans. Stephen Corrin. New York: Harper & Row, 1971.

———. "The Myth of Alchemy." *Parabola: Myth and the Quest for Meaning* 3, no. 3 (August 1979):7–23.

———. *The Myth of the Eternal Return.* Trans. Willard R. Trask. Princeton, N.J.: Princeton University Press, 1971.

———. *The Quest: History and Meaning in Religion.* Chicago: University of Chicago Press, 1975.

———. *The Sacred and the Profane: The Nature of Religion.* Trans. Willard R. Trask. New York: Harcourt Brace Jovanovich, 1968.

Estess, Ted. "The 'Inenarrable Contraption': Reflections on the Metaphor of Story." *Journal of the American Academy of Religion* 42, no. 3 (September 1974):415–34.

Fox, Matthew. *Original Blessing: A Primer in Creation Spirituality.* Santa Fe, N.Mex.: Bear and Company, 1986.

Holt, David. "Projection, Presence, Profession." *Spring* (1975):130–45.

Hopper, Stanley. "Reports and Prophecies in the Literature of Our Time." *The Christian Scholar* 40, no. 4 (December 1957):312–30.

Hopper, Stanley, and David L. Miller, eds. *Interpretation: The Poetry of Meaning.* New York: Harcourt Brace Jovanovich, 1967.

Joyce, James. *A Portrait of the Artist as a Young Man.* New York: Penguin Books, 1987.

Kluckhorn, Clyde. "Recurrent Themes in Myths and Mythmaking." In *Myth and Mythmaking,* ed. Henry A. Murray. New York: George Braziller, Inc., 1960, 46–60.

Merleau-Ponty, Maurice. *Sense and Non-Sense.* Trans. Hubert and Patricia Dreyfus. Evanston, Ill.: Northwestern University Press, 1964.

———. *The Visible and the Invisible: Followed by Working Notes.* Trans. Alphonso Lingis. Ed. Claude Lefort. Evanston, Ill.: Northwestern University Press, 1968.

Noel, Daniel C., ed. *Echoes of the Wordless "Word."* Ithaca, N.Y.: Scholars Press, 1974.

Onians, R. B. *Origins of European Thought.* Cambridge: Cambridge University Press, 1954.

Ovid. *Metamorphoses.* Trans. Rolfe Humphries. Bloomington, Inc.: Indiana University Press, 1958.

Pagels, Elaine. "The Gnostic Vision." *Parabola* 3, no. 4 (1978):6–10.

Steiner, George. *Language and Silence: Essays on Language, Literature and Film.* New York: Atheneum Press, 1967.

Wheelwright, Philip. *Metaphor and Reality.* Bloomington, Ind.: Indiana University Press, 1968.

Wiggins, James B. "Within and Without Stories." In his edition, *Religion as Story.* New York: Harper & Row, 1975, 1–22.

Yates, Frances A. *Giordano Bruno and the Hermetic Tradition.* London: Routledge & Kegan Paul, 1964.

V. Other Related Sources

The American Heritage Dictionary of the English Language. Ed. William Morris. New York: Houghton Mifflin Co., 1969.

The Analects of Confucius. Trans. Arthur Waley. London: G. Allen & Union Ltd., 1949.

Bell, Clive. *Aesthetics and Post-Impressionaism: A New Theory of Art.* London: Chatto and Windus, 1949.

Camus, Albert. *The Myth of Sisyphus and Other Essays.* Trans. Justin O'Brien. New York: Alfred A. Knopf, 1955.

————. *The Plague.* Trans. Gilbert Stuart. New York: Random House, 1969.

Dante Alighieri. *The Divine Comedy.* Trans. John D. Sinclair. New York: Oxford University Press, 1961.

Derrida, Jacques. "Living On." In *Deconstruction and Criticism.* New York: Continuum Pub. Co., 1979, 75–176.

"The Homeric Hymn to Demeter." In *The Homeric Hymns and Homerica.* Trans. G. Evelyn-White. Cambridge, Mass.: Harvard University Press, 1964, 288–323.

Langer, Suzanne. *Feeling and Form.* New York: Scribners and Co., 1953.

Merchant, Carolyn. *Death of Nature: Women, Ecology, and the Scientific Revolution.* New York: Harper & Row, 1983.

Miller, J. Hillis. "The Critic as Host." In *Deconstruction and Criticism.* New York: Continuum Pub. Co., 1979, 217–54.

Olson, Charles. "Proprioception." In *Charles Olson: Additional Prose.* Ed. George Butterick. Bolinas, Calif.: Four Seasons Press, 1974.

Plato. *Phaedrus.* Trans. R. Hackforth. New York: Cambridge University Press, 1972.

Prigogine, Ilya, and Isabelle Stengers. *Order Out of Chaos: Man's New Dialogue with Nature.* New York: Bantam Press, 1984.

Saussure, Ferdinand de. "Langue et parole." In *Cours de la linguistique générale.* Paris: Payot, 1961.

Index

BECKETT AND MYTH

was composed in 10 and 12 Goudy Old Style on a Mergenthaler Linotron 202
by Partners Composition,
with display type in Baker Signet by Dix Type, Inc.,
printed by sheet-fed offset on 60-pound acid-free Glatfelter Natural Hi Bulk,
Smyth sewn and bound over binder's boards in Holliston Roxite B,
with dust jackets printed in two colors by Braun-Brumfield, Inc.;
and published by
Syracuse University Press
Syracuse, New York 13244-5160